INTELLIGENCE WAS MY LINE

INTELLIGENCE WAS MY LINE: INSIDE EISENHOWER'S OTHER COMMAND

As told to Donald E. Markle by

Colonel Ralph W. Hauenstein, *Chief,*

Intelligence Branch (G-2), Hq., ETOUSA

01/29/07

To Jim —
m fellow
Goard member & good
friend, [signature]

HIPPOCRENE BOOKS, INC.
New York

Copyright © 2005 Ralph Hauenstein & Donald Markle.
First Edition, Hippocrene Books, 2005.

Book design by Susan A. Ahlquist.
Jacket design by Ronnie McBride.

Hippocrene Books
171 Madison Avenue
New York, NY 10016
www.hippocrenebooks.com

ISBN 0-7818-1117-1

Cataloging-in-Publication data available from the Library of Congress.

Printed in the United States of America.

This book is dedicated to my family,
whose love and devotion to me far exceeds,
to the fullest measure,
those services I performed during the war years.

—Ralph W. Hauenstein

In the work of intelligence, heroes are undecorated and unsung, often even among their own fraternity. Their inspiration is rooted in patriotism, their reward can be little except the convictions that they are performing a unique and indispensable service for their country and the knowledge that America needs and appreciates their efforts.

—Dwight D. Eisenhower,
Langley, Virginia,
November 3, 1959

Contents

Contents

Introduction

Donald E. Markle

The experiences of veterans of World War II have been well documented among two very specific groups—senior commanders (through biographies and memoirs) and the common soldier (through the writings of historians such as Stephen Ambrose). But there is another group, which I call the "worker-bee" level of officers, not well represented for modern readers. They and the organizations to which they were assigned, such as the European Theater of Operations, U.S. Army, known as ETOUSA, have earned no more than a comment in the histories of the period.

These men and women and their organizations were responsible for putting the overall strategy and plans of the senior commanders into effect on a daily basis, and ensuring that all the needs of the armies involved in the tactical phase of the war were met. This was not an easy job, and, yes, they were in the shadows: they did not capture towns, take prisoners, advance 10 miles in a day, or perform any other heroic act that became fodder for the newspapers. They were the shadow element, always in the background, quietly supporting the fighting forces.

Ralph W. Hauenstein is one of these officers, and the organization he was assigned to—ETOUSA—is one of the phantoms of the U.S. Army war effort in Europe. Rising to the rank of colonel, Hauenstein served as the chief of the Intelligence Branch (G-2) for the European Theater of Operations, United States Army, from late 1943 until late summer of 1945. His experiences in Iceland and later with ETOUSA in support of the U.S. tactical elements in Europe have until recently remained only a personal memory, not shared with anyone. Now his story can and should be told.

After being assigned with the forward group to Iceland in the late summer of 1941, he was later reassigned to ETOUSA in London,

England, arriving in August of 1943. He soon moved into the G-2 (operations) at ETOUSA headquarters, assisting in intelligence work, and was later assigned full time to the intelligence branch, where he became chief in late 1943. He served in that capacity until he returned to the States in the late summer of 1945.

As chief of the Intelligence Branch, G-2, he was a key player in the intelligence operations of both the United States Army (ETOUSA) and the Supreme Headquarters Allied Expeditionary Forces (SHAEF); as such, he was involved in the day-to-day operations of the Allied forces in Europe. And until 1998 he never spoke a word to anyone about what he had done there, what he knew, or what he did not know. He was all too aware that some of his experiences remained highly classified long after the war, and he was not going to jeopardize the U.S. for his personal aggrandizement.

As an intelligence officer in the U.S. Army during World War II, he could not keep a daily diary of what occurred in his area of operations—it was against Army regulations. Ralph himself says, and he is right, that had this book been undertaken immediately after World War II, it would have told a very different story, one that, if richer in minutiae, would have been poorer in perspective and analysis. The stories he recounts here are the 50-year-old memories of a very sharp individual who looks upon his experiences as a duty, nothing more than that. In fact, however, they are more than just that. His memories fill in some of the blanks of history, offering a new perspective on some of the military efforts in Europe during World War II.

During our discussions of his military career, it became very obvious that Colonel Hauenstein, who retired from the Army Reserve with his wartime rank, felt that several important phases of World War II had not been treated fairly or correctly by historians. The first example was the prewar deployment of U.S. forces to Iceland. The second was the U.S. Command known as the European Theater of Operations, U.S. Army (ETOUSA), established by General Eisenhower at the direction of General George Marshall as the single command element for the U.S. Army. ETOUSA receives virtually no credit or acknowledgement for its role in the war in Europe. The third came in response to the question, "Just what did General Eisenhower know about the nuclear program in the United States and when did he know it?" Colonel Hauenstein's experiences reflect on all of the above areas.

Introduction

It has been fascinating to talk with a man who was "there" for many of the major decisions of the Second World War in Europe—a man who had and still has a strong sense of history, a keen perspective on the personalities around him, and a good sense of humor, but above all is an American and proud of it.

In the text, I have chosen a format that couples the memories of Colonel Hauenstein with additional historical facts in footnotes. I hope that the reader will thus be able to see the background of actions, as well as the results, which were often out of Colonel Hauenstein's control. The impact of those war years remains with Colonel Hauenstein today, as reflected in a speech he gave recently, included here in an epilogue.

In conclusion, let me say that Ralph W. Hauenstein did not pull in his oars after his Army career but continued to succeed in his endeavors in both private and government sectors. It has been my extreme pleasure to know Ralph; he epitomizes a generation of Americans that without hesitation rose to the Nazi challenge to American democracy, won the challenge, and then quietly went back to the civilian sector without any demand for praise or glory.

—Donald E. Markle
Gettysburg, Pennsylvania, 2005

Intelligence Was My Line

Storm Clouds

October 1940

I was at my city editor desk at the *Grand Rapids Herald* when a telegram arrived that changed my life forever. Opening it, I saw that I was being called to active duty as a first lieutenant in the United States Army. As an Army reservist, I was not totally surprised. Yes, it meant leaving my family to serve, and though I could not help but recall the past events that led me to this juncture and contemplate the future, it was my duty to my country. It might require separation from my young family for an indefinite amount of time, but I did have the solace of knowing that my wife, Grace, was in this with me all the way—as many American wives were discovering at this perilous time. How did this all happen?

The time was the late 1930s. The storm clouds of war were gathering over Europe, and as the city editor I knew it. Every day, reports from all over the world came across my desk, providing me a current "snapshot" of events far beyond the local interests of Grand Rapids readers—but of great interest to me. How did I happen to be in such an advantageous spot while still in my early twenties? My story is typical of the great depression period of American history.

I was born in Indiana on 20 March 1912, the youngest of three sons. At the age of 12, I moved with my family back to Grand Rapids, which has been my permanent home since that time. My family had been early settlers in Michigan, with varying degrees of prosperity. My ancestors were proud Americans, as exemplified by two who served as lieutenants in the Revolutionary War and my paternal grandfather who fought in the Civil War. After graduating from high school, I attended the local college where, during a summer break, I worked as a copy boy at the *Grand Rapids Press*. This short stint started me on the path to a newspaper career. I was hired as night police reporter, and what an experience that was! This was the era of prohibition, bootlegging, members of the Purple Gang (a group of mobsters from Detroit), and riots. It was a pretty freewheeling society. During this period I also worked for United Press International and was a stringer for several publications, including the *Christian Science Monitor*, which paid the highest per inch for published material. When I received a commission as second lieutenant in the Army Reserve (nonactive duty), I soon volunteered for a 30-month tour in the Civilian Conservation Corps (CCC). Upon completion of the CCC assignment, my strong desire to return to newspaper work led me to the *Grand Rapids Herald* where, within a year, I became its city editor. In this position, I was a bit in awe of several of my predecessors, such as Frank Knox, who later became editor of the *Chicago Daily News* and then the World War II Secretary of the Navy, as well as Arthur Vandenberg, who rose to be editor of the newspaper and later senator from Michigan.

The period proved to be a very active one for a newspaperman, and I soon learned the art of working with the police, their informants, and tipsters to develop a story. What I was unwittingly learning was the art of developing "all-source intelligence." Little did I then know how this would play out in my later life.

The work was great; I loved it and did a rather good job of it. But the work did not so totally encompass me that I did not have time for a personal life. I was a young man who enjoyed female companionship, and I soon found one particular lady whose company was very special to me. Her name was Grace Byrnes, a student nurse in Grand Rapids. Our friendship grew into a love that still exists today. Each year since 1932 we celebrate our wedding anniversary on the 31st of March. I will always consider that date the luckiest day of my life.

Life was good, but by the mid-1930s I became more and more aware that military and political events in Europe, as well as in Asia, did not bode well for the future. It appeared that there was a growing probability of another world war exploding on the free world and that men my age would be called on once again to protect the free world from evil forces. Service to one's country in times of conflict was a family tradition for the Hauensteins: I had no doubt that I would enter the Army. I decided it was better to serve as an officer, and so I proceeded along that course. In 1934 I took the series of examinations (academic and physical) required to become a U.S. Army Reserve officer. I passed and was given a commission as second lieutenant. Thus began my Army career.

Ralph Hauenstein, seated at the city editor desk of the Grand Rapids Herald, *1938. His experience here later proved invaluable in his role as a military intelligence officer in World War II. The other man in the background is Jim Hitchcock, the news editor.*

At this juncture I had no idea how my life would play out or that the early experiences I had at the newspaper would have such a critical role in my Army career. I already knew how to develop "information" and turn it into "intelligence"; it was just the readership that would be different. In lieu of civilian professionals, I would be reporting to senior Army officers, to include four-star generals at the highest level of military service.

Civilian Conservation Corps (CCC)

May 1935 to November 1937

When I joined the U.S. Army Reserve as a second lieutenant, I remained in the newspaper business, but it soon became clear that it would be only a matter of time before I, too, would be formally engaged in the defense of my country. With this in mind, and with my wife's blessing, I volunteered in May of 1935 for a two-and-a-half-year active-duty assignment with the Civilian Conservation Corps (CCC) in Michigan. This, my initial active duty assignment, was a real eye-opener for me in the ways of the military and another culture.

The CCC was established in 1933 by the Franklin D. Roosevelt administration to provide employment for young men who, because of the depression, were unable to find work. Michigan was part of the 6th Corps of the CCC, with headquarters in Chicago. The mission of the Michigan CCC troops was predominately forestation and restoration of parklands, which included the planting of trees, the creation of roads and trails in park areas, and the establishment of new park and recreational facilities.

The CCC's efforts in my state encompassed 27,000 men in 59 separate camps, with a total of 139 camps in the 6th Corps area overall. One specific target group recruited for the Corps was World War I veterans who were assigned to special camps; in Michigan, there were five World War I camps. About 10% of the recruits were World War I veterans, and an equal number were black, African-American veterans (then known as "colored").

I wondered, why such an assignment? What I did not know at the time was that the Army was using the CCC as a training ground for its officers, particularly those destined to be military intelligence officers. During the early 1930s the Army arranged:

- Active duty with the CCC for 117 military intelligence officers (all field grade)

7

- Assignment of active-duty company grade officers to the CCC in 1935

- Placement of reserve officers on extended active duty with the CCC (in 1935)

While these personnel were seldom given any specific intelligence duties to perform, they did obtain a great deal of practical experience that later turned out to be an invaluable asset for all concerned.

In 1935 I was one of the reserve officer cadres deployed to the Michigan CCC for duty and experience. My military on-the-job training had begun! One of my first tasks consisted of being given a transit and a tripod, with an order to go out into the Michigan wilderness and set up a camp within a specified deadline. I hardly knew which end of a transit to look through at that point—but I did meet the deadline.

The deadline was the day that the camp would be receiving 160 of what were then called colored veterans. They were all residents of Michigan. It was the national policy, throughout the entire CCC period (1933–1942), to have all camps segregated, even though many attempts were made by the various states participating in the program to integrate them. Working with these veterans was a baptism by fire, as I was initially totally unprepared for the job. These veterans knew every trick in the book and then some. I was a 23-year-old yearling, who knew all too few tricks. That assignment taught me many lessons that have remained with me throughout my life, not all of which resulted from the actions of the black troops—I learned a great deal about the whole issue of segregation, as well.

I had grown up in a predominately white neighborhood and I was totally unaware of the racial issues fermenting at that time in Michigan. But, boy, did I learn. For example, we had a town nearby, and one of the things our camp recruits wanted to do was to go to town on Saturday and watch a movie. Sounds simple, but my black troops were not allowed in the local theater. Soon enough with a little negotiation, the CCC boys were allowed into the movie theater—though only in the balcony.

One of my first colored camps—the U.S. Army official title for such camps—was designated the 670th, the first all-black unit in Michigan. It was initially located at Camp Bitely in the Manistee National Forest, where we spent a short time while preparing a new camp site at Walkerville. Once the camps were up and running, my duties consisted of functioning as first a deputy camp commander and mess officer and later as a camp commander. My job was to ensure that camp discipline was maintained and that our projects were completed.

Both of these locations were near Idlewild, a famous resort where people of color from all over the midwest came for their summer vacations and where famous black entertainers came to perform.[1] Occasionally, for special events, I would take a truckload or two of my men over to Idlewild to visit. My presence was necessary, as Army regulations required that an officer accompany the men on such excursions, and since all our officers were white, we would accompany the trucks. I will always remember that, although I might have been the only white man in that crowd—my men, the resort visitors, and the entertainers, as well as the locals—I was always well and respectfully treated. Our camp flourished, and I learned a lot about the administrative functions of a military command structure. When my commanding officer came to visit our camp, he decided to address the troops to instill them with pride in a job well done. Accustomed to commanding white troops, he made an inadvertent slip in his speech. Suddenly aware of his mistake, he abruptly turned the platform over to me and beat a quick retreat. I learned rank has its privileges.

The camps proved highly valuable in the training of officers, and after World War II, General George C. Marshall reported that it was the CCC that provided the army with its officer leadership.

One of the greatest challenges as the second-in-command officer was the assignment of mess officer. It was not an easy task, given an allocation of 12 cents per man per meal per day, which was all we had to feed men who had been working all day planting trees, building bridges, and performing other physically hard labor. Certain staples such as beans, flour, and sugar could be ordered from the commissary, and the remainder we purchased on the open market. The meals were well balanced, and complaints were rare. I became aware of the special tastes of my troops and tried to accommodate them as much as possible. For example, when the inspector general came from Chicago to investigate some complaints of "poor food," he found that what my black troops really wanted was black-eyed peas and neck bones; this was the diet to which they were accustomed. Adjustments were duly made.

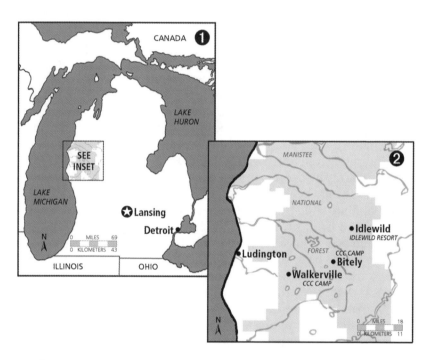

Civilian Conservation Corps (CCC) camps at Walkerville and Bitely and the Idlewild resort.

While my duties were varied, they became routine, although I was sometimes challenged in unfamiliar ways. When fights broke out among my troops over a variety of reasons, including money, work habits, and possible thefts, I was called on to break them up. This proved to be a real challenge, as I never knew if either of the combatants was armed or what the weapon might be.

I served in the CCC for two years and six months, from May of 1935 to November of 1937, in both white and black camps. My experiences with black veterans were an exposure to a new culture—as it later would be for many Americans during the war years to come when soldiers of color became an integral part of the U.S. Army. The time was well spent, both personally and professionally. I learned not only how to be a troop commander but also how to deal with another culture, and our camp was very productive in completing our assigned tasks. To this day I can drive proudly through areas of Michigan that were forested by my CCC troops.

Subsequent to my departure from the CCC, its role changed. With war clouds starting to gather on the horizon, President Roosevelt declared a limited national emergency in late 1940, and CCC camps became part of the national defense effort and were to construct military projects.

My CCC days ended with the expiration of my tour of duty, and my family, who had followed me to my CCC locations, moved back to Grand Rapids. I returned to the newspaper business, joining the editorial staff of another Grand Rapids newspaper, the *Grand Rapids Herald*, and shortly became the city editor—but not for long. In December of 1940, I returned to active duty with the regular Army.

The CCC had given me the leadership experiences I needed to fill the boots of a military officer, yet I was only 28 years old and was leaving behind a wife and three children to face what could best be described as an uncertain future. The stakes were high, but so was my determination to succeed, and it was with a heart full of resolve that I made the trip to Fort Sheridan, Illinois.

NOTE

1. Among the famous entertainers who performed at Idlewild were Duke Ellington, Louis Armstrong, Sarah Vaughan, and Count Basie, along with Joe Louis, the boxer, and Dr. Daniel H. Williams, the pioneering Chicago heart surgeon. The site also attracted poet playwright Langston Hughes, novelist Zora Neale Hurston, and the co-founder of the NAACP W. E. B. DuBois.

Fort Sheridan

December 1940 to August 1941

On 15 December 1940 I went on active duty with the United States Army with an assignment to Fort Sheridan, Illinois. Based on my civilian newspaper experience, I was assigned to the S-2 (intelligence) section on the staff of Colonel John L. Homer, a West Point graduate who had previously served on the staff of General Marshall. I was assigned as the public affairs officer. (At that time the public affairs officer was an integral part of the S-2 staff and not a separate staff group.) Fort Sheridan was the home base for one of the few anti-aircraft artillery (AAA) units in the Army inventory.

At this point my Army life changed drastically. I was no longer the company commander of a group of CCC recruits or the city editor of a newspaper; I was now serving in the military as an individual member of a staff element. It was a natural fit; I was back in the information business with only one difference—I now wore a uniform and was reporting to a different audience. I had learned many lessons as a camp commander, and now I could meld those with my newspaper experience to really function in a role beneficial to the U.S. Army.

Military intelligence was an area whose importance was not quite as pronounced during times of peace, as in times of war, which accounted for the dual responsibilities—intelligence and public relations—for members of the S-2 section. When I arrived at Fort Sheridan, the officer in charge of the S-2 staff was a former FBI agent. Colonel Homer assigned me this man's position because I was of a higher rank, but public relations were more appealing to me, and so I told my fellow officer that he could control the intelligence area while I focused on the former.

The role of public affairs officers was not easy, as the country was in a state of pronounced turmoil regarding the question of war. Isolationists such as Charles Lindbergh and members of the America

13

First Committee had created a blitz of antiwar rhetoric that was rising to a fevered pitch. Citizens objected to sending American boys to fight in—or even train for—what they regarded as a European conflict. The scars of World War I were still too fresh for Yanks to rally behind the idea of another "war to end all wars," and politicians had not been eager to ruffle the public's feathers. Because of this widespread outcry against mobilization, the military had been poorly equipped, with archaic uniforms and weapons to match. Fort Sheridan itself was being used as a whipping post by members of the local Chicago press, who wished to berate the Army for its lack of equipment and organization. Finger-pointing against the U.S. military became a national sport.

To counter this negative attitude, I decided to take some positive steps. First, being a former newspaperman, I established a Fort Sheridan newspaper for the troops stationed there. It carried some national news but concentrated on activities inside the base, sports results, promotion reports, family news, and anything else of interest to the men. The newspaper had a very positive effect on the morale of the troops.

At the same time I was performing S-2 functions, I was conducting a project known as Counter-Subversive, by which units down to the company level were reporting on possible subversive individuals in the military, in particular in their own units. The plan required one individual in each company to report (by confidential letter to my office) any unusual activities that could be considered subversive.

My early intelligence work focused mainly on the world around me at Fort Sheridan, and often my covert actions centered very close to home. For example, soon after my arrival, I came to discover that the only reason my commander, Colonel Homer, had not been promoted to brigadier general was that a few months earlier a fire of unknown origin had occurred in a garage on one of his posts. Colonel Homer's promotion was being held up pending an investigation of this incident, and I found the case file on my desk. After reading the file, I contacted the FBI for assistance. The responding agent quickly determined that an off-duty driver had started the fire by smoking a cigarette while siphoning gasoline for his personal use. I'm not sure whether Colonel Homer gave the credit for finding the culprit to the FBI or to me, but in any case it was only a matter of weeks before he received his star and became a brigadier general.

Not long after my assignment as the public affairs officer at Fort Sheridan, the U.S. Army made some major changes in its public affairs procedures. With the probability of another war increasing, the Army wanted a more effective interface between the military and the civilian press. This would help both the military morale and in no small way prevent the constant circulating of rumors. In February of 1941, the Secretary of War established the Bureau of Public Relations (BPR). The BPR was to be independent from the Military Intelligence Department (MID), which was tasked with interfacing between the military and the public press. One of the first actions of the BPR was to sponsor a conference, in Washington, D.C., to determine the role of the new organization and its coordination with the MID. As the public affairs officer at Fort Sheridan, and one of the few in the country, I participated in the conference.

The conference, held in February of 1941, was total chaos. Many of the attendees wore not only public affairs hats but military intelligence ones as well—two masters! I recall speaking with BPR director Brigadier General Robert Richardson and with noted columnist Walter Lippman about the problem of public affairs versus military intelligence. I vividly recall a story Mr. Lippman told me to show how publicity and intelligence can successfully work together—not separately—if they were well coordinated.

The story told by Mr. Lippman occurred during the World War I era. It seems that a German radio program, widely monitored in London, made an announcement concerning Big Ben, the clock over the British Parliament building. The transmission, heard by many, stated that at that exact moment, Big Ben was a couple minutes slow. As you would expect, all London looked to Big Ben, and sure enough it was exactly three minutes slow! Londoners were appalled; how would the Germans know that? They must have agents everywhere. So this was a very deft move: it was a simple but effective use of psychological warfare. That was the highlight of the conference for me. Beyond that, it appeared that each public affairs officer would have to make his own way in establishing himself with the military intelligence folks, so that is exactly what I did.

My duties as public affairs officer at Fort Sheridan varied, and one of my real coups, so to speak, occurred in the spring of 1941. Colonel Robert R. McCormack, the owner of the *Chicago Tribune*, was constantly complaining in his newspaper about the U.S. Army's apparent lack of preparedness. I suggested that we bring the colonel to Fort

Sheridan and stage a review in his honor, with as many troops as possible and lots of equipment rolling by, which could be expanded by having some units and equipment passing more than once, switching unit banners each time. He accepted. Upon his arrival at Fort Sheridan, a great show was put on in his honor, and the U.S. Army never heard another word from him about the preparedness of the U.S. Army. The famous Colonel McCormack had been duped by one of the oldest tricks in the military bag of tricks.

Being curious by nature, I searched the files at Fort Sheridan for manuals or precedents to follow in my development of intelligence. There were none. It was all done by the seat of the pants. It was left to each individual S-2 staff member to develop an intelligence structure for its specific command. Military intelligence staffing at that time was very minimal. In 1940, for example, there were only 28 officers, 3 enlisted men, and 49 civilians in the MID; by the end of 1941 those numbers had increased to 200 officers, 0 enlisted men, and 648 civilians. Things were changing.

Here again, my experience with the newspaper proved invaluable—I knew how to collect information and how to present it for the best effect. My techniques were my own and, at that point, not incorporated into any formal structure at all.

Life at Fort Sheridan had become a steady stream of marching drills, weapons training, and similar military exercises. It was routine and somewhat dull, until, in the early summer of 1941, an exciting event took place at Fort Sheridan. The fort received one of the first radars to control AAA gunfire, the SCR-268. It was sent to Fort Sheridan as we had one of the few AAA units in the Army inventory. The equipment, state-of-the-art at the time, was complex and required quite a learning curve. The SCR-268 was not the class sent to Pearl Harbor prior to the attack—that was the SCR-270 specifically designed to spot aircraft. Many countries had been experimenting with the radar technology. It was the U.K. that provided the technology for the magnetron oscillator (in 1940), thus allowing the U.S. to successfully create both the SCR-268 and SCR-270. The U.K. had provided the magnetron technology as a quid for the U.S. providing the cryptanalytic techniques for the breaking of the Japanese diplomatic code, which the U.S. called PURPLE.

Our troops soon discovered a major flaw when operating the equipment. The wheels on which the SCR-268 moved kept falling off or malfunctioning. The tenor of the times immediately said sabotage

16

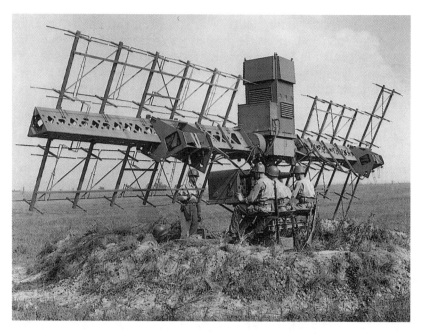

The SCR-268 anti-aircraft radar was one of the first developed by the U.S. Signal Corps. The first models, built by Western Electric, were delivered in February of 1941. They had a beam width of 2 degrees vertical and horizontal and a distance capability of 36 kilometers (23 miles).

was at work, and a massive investigation was initiated to get to the bottom of the problem. The final result of the investigation was that the problem resulted from faulty manufacturing of the ball bearings, not from sabotage. Once the correction was made, all was well.

But in the early summer of 1941 great excitement arose over the SCR-268; had it been compromised? While the subject of radar was still highly classified and very hush-hush, a Buck Rogers comic strip appeared showing Buck shooting down an enemy aircraft using radar! As even the term "radar" was classified, this caused a major flap. I had to go to Chicago to be questioned by the Illinois FBI office regarding possible leaks regarding radar and the SCR-268 at Fort Sheridan. It caused a storm of investigations and worry, and I never did hear the final outcome of the FBI investigation or see the strip in question.

While I was serving at Fort Sheridan, events were taking place in Washington, D.C., that would soon affect my Army career. As I was to later learn, U.S. Army forces were about to be deployed in Iceland to prevent a German takeover of the island. All I knew in the summer of 1941 was that Brigadier General John Homer, the commander at Fort Sheridan, had been ordered by Washington to embark on a highly classified mission assignment. For the early stages of this assignment, he and his staff would remain at Fort Sheridan.

In August of 1941, at General Homer's request, I was assigned to a U.S. Army unit whose existence was top secret—the United States had not yet entered the war. We were to be transferred to Iceland to relieve the U.S. Marines, who, in turn, had relieved the British Army who had been in Iceland since 8 May 1940. I was the public affairs officer in the G-2[1] section of an Army element that did not exist. The assignment was a direct result of General Homer's knowledge of my work on his staff at Fort Sheridan. In his new position as chief of staff, Iceland Base Command, he needed staff officers of proven capability to him. He could depend on these officers to handle the unique tasks associated with a U.S. Army serving abroad on a wartime status but not in a war.

At this point, my geographic separation from my family increased by leaps and bounds. Fort Sheridan was not that great a distance from Grand Rapids, enabling me to still spend some time with my family. But with the new assignment, that was about to come to an abrupt halt. My wife, like many other American wives, would have total responsibility for raising our three children as long as the war continued. I was fortunate; I knew my wife was a very capable woman who could assume this role almost without missing a beat. That was a great comfort to me and allowed me to concentrate on my own mission.

NOTE

1. Staff officers below division level are designated by the letter S, above division level by the letter G.

Iceland, General Background

1941

When General Homer was relieved of his command at Fort Sheridan and assigned to a special project in the summer of 1941, I had no idea that I would soon be joining him. For the initial phase of the project, General Homer remained physically located at Fort Sheridan and did so until the troops began to assemble in New York just prior to their movement to Iceland in September of 1941.

General Homer had to assemble a staff of officers to accompany him on this assignment, and I was selected to join his staff as the public affairs officer in the office of the G-2. Only then did I become aware of what the highly classified "special project" encompassed—it all revolved around Iceland.

Being an ex–investigative reporter and a current public affairs officer, I immediately began to receive briefings on the mission and soon received the answer to my question, "Why Iceland?" It became very clear to me why U.S. troops were being deployed to such a remote spot, and why it had to be done under a cloak of security.

From a military point of view, Iceland occupied a very important strategic location in the North Atlantic, particularly against a power that was using submarine warfare so effectively. As I studied further, I found that Germans had been in Iceland as early as 1928–1931, surveying and photographing the island. They strategically placed markers on lava plateaus to guide future aircraft landings. More recently, in 1939, Germany had sent her warship the *Emden* on a "courtesy" visit to Reykjavik and asked for preferential air base rights, a request to which the government of Iceland promptly said, "No!" Later it emerged that Germany had a plan known as Project IKARUS for the invasion of Iceland. The Icelandic government was aware that Germany had become a threat.

One of my first undertakings was to look at the geography of Iceland. As I did, it became obvious why the U.S. and England were so interested: both wanted control of the North Atlantic Ocean. This location was a prime concern of the British, who were so dependent on activities under the Lend-Lease Act. Their survival rested on Allied control of Iceland. If Iceland fell into German hands, the sea lanes between the U.S. and England, which were the lifeline for the survival of Britain, would be in jeopardy. Iceland also had another important asset since, unlike Greenland, where the ports are frozen over more than half the year, the ports of Iceland are generally free of ice packs year-round. Ships could use the ports as they transited the Atlantic, and this was a critical factor for emergency repairs or refueling. Affairs began to fall into place.

As I learned more about the current status of Iceland, I realized that the situation had been brewing for some time at the governmental level but not for the general American public. The Iceland question had begun while the British were smarting over the fall of Europe to the Germans in 1940. They were already wary of their own future, when in the spring of 1940 their intelligence service reported the gathering of forces in Norway for an invasion of Iceland.[1] The British were quick to realize the significance of the island, and in May/June of 1940, they "occupied" the entire country of Iceland in order to prevent a German occupation.[2] It was a relief to learn that the Icelandic people had chosen not to contest the "occupation," as it had provided needed protection for their country. In all probability, our entry into Iceland to replace the British troops would also be viewed in a positive way by the Icelandic population. But at the same time, it would not go unnoticed by the Germans.

I subsequently learned that, simultaneously with the U.K. occupation, discussions commenced between the British and the Americans leading to the understanding that the U.S. would take responsibility for Iceland if and when we entered the war. As fighting progressed in Europe, the British increased pressure on the U.S. to move into Iceland and release the U.K. contingent to defend its own homeland. All of the Army public affairs officers of the time knew that the U.S. was striving to remain neutral, and it seemed we would withstand the U.K. pressure. However, the continued reporting of the presence of the large German army concentration in Norway, presumably poised to invade Iceland, changed minds in Washington. The threat to U.S. ships crossing the Atlantic had become too real to ignore.

At this point, intelligence led the U.S. to deploy a U.S. destroyer, the USS *Niblack* (DD-424) on a mission of armed reconnaissance in Icelandic waters to protect Allied shipping. On 10 April 1941 the *Niblack* rescued three boatloads of Dutch seaman who had survived the German U-boat sinking of their ship the *Saleier*. During the rescue the *Niblack* detected a possible U-boat attack on their ship, and the *Niblack* responded with depth charges. I recall the day we received the news of the possible attack on the *Niblack* as it marked the first engagement between Nazi naval vessels and the United States. The event was highly reported by the U.S. press.

Following this event, the U.S. opened negotiations with Thor Thors, the Icelandic consul general in Washington, about a U.S. military presence in Iceland. The talks were so restricted that neither Secretary of State Cordell Hull nor the British ambassador Lord Edward Halifax knew about them.

When in June of 1941 the U.K. informed the Icelandic government that Britain could no longer provide troops to protect Iceland from invasion by the Germans, the U.K. government was still unaware of the U.S. negotiations. They further suggested to the Icelandic government that U.S. troops might be sent to replace U.K. men, if so requested. The prime minister of Iceland, Hermann Jonasson, agreed but avoided the use of the word "invite," as that would have required the permission of the Icelandic Parliament. Consequently, a message was sent to President Roosevelt containing the following passage:

> In a conversation of June 24 the British Minister explained the immense importance of adequate defense of Iceland. He also called my attention to the declaration of the President of the United States to the effect that he must take all necessary measure to assist in the defense of Iceland—and that the President is therefore prepared to send immediately United States troops to replace the British force here. But that he does not consider that he can take this course except at the invitation of the Icelandic Government.
>
> After careful consideration of all the circumstances, the Icelandic Government, in view of the present state of affairs, admit that this measure is in accordance with the interest of Iceland, and therefore are ready to entrust the protection of Iceland to United States on the following conditions.[3]

Based on the two requests, one from the U.K. and one from Iceland, President Roosevelt on 7 July 1941 sent a message to Congress in which he announced the following:

* * * * *

The United States cannot permit the occupation by Germany of strategic outposts in the Atlantic to be used as air or naval bases for eventual attack against the Western Hemisphere. We have no desire to see any change in the present sovereignty of those regions. Assurance that such outposts in our defense-frontier remain in friendly hands is the very foundation of our national security and of every one of the independent nations of the New World.

For the same reason substantial forces of the United States have now been sent to the bases acquired last year from Great Britain in Trinidad and in British Guiana in the south in order to forestall any pincers movement undertaken by Germany against the Western Hemisphere. It is essential that Germany should not be able successfully to employ such tactics through sudden seizures of strategic points in the South Atlantic and in the North Atlantic.

* * * * *

The occupation of Iceland would constitute a serious threat in three dimensions:

- The threat against Greenland and the northern portion of the North American Continent, including the islands which lie off it.

- The threat against all shipping in the North Atlantic.

- The threat against the steady flow of munitions to Britain—which is a matter of broad policy clearly approved by Congress.

It is therefore imperative that the approaches between the Americas and those strategic outposts, the safety of which this country regards as essential to its national security, and which it must therefore defend, shall remain open and free from all hostile activity or threat thereof.

24

As Commander in Chief I have consequently issued orders to the Navy that all necessary steps be taken to insure the safety of communications in the approaches between Iceland and the United States, as well as on the seas between the United States and all other strategic outposts.

This Government will ensure the adequate defense of Iceland with full recognition of the independence of Iceland as a sovereign state.[4]

The President's message was well received by Congress, and, according to a Gallup poll taken on 17 July 1941, the American population, by a percentage of 61%, approved of the move to a "dynamic defense." While in agreement with the president's action, I did not realize how it would soon affect my military career.

Once the decision was made to replace the British troops in Iceland with U.S. troops, several major administrative and legal problems still remained to be solved. For troop selection, first and foremost was one of the restrictions placed on the deployment of selectees (draftees). By presidential directive they could not be used in defense of the U.S. Atlantic coast east of the 26th meridian. Iceland was located east of that line. Second, Congress had passed a law that Selective Service personnel would serve for only one year and then be released. Hence it would have been impossible to assemble the command structure using selectees since the turnover would be so great for an expedition going overseas—it would abort the project. Therefore the U.S. troops to be deployed to Iceland had to be regular Army personnel; this was not a major problem for the officer corps but was a significant one for the enlisted personnel. The loss of a large contingent of regular Army troops would have a detrimental effect on the increasing demand for veteran troops to train the selectees.

General Marshall was actively involved in the selection of the troops for Iceland. He was determined to place U.S. Army troops as close to the European continent as possible. They would serve as the vanguard of U.S. troops that he was certain would be deployed to Europe in the near future.

A second problem was the massive supply requirements, both initial and sustained. The initial estimate called for transporting approximately 29,000 men and 231,000 ship tons of supplies. The normal resupply effort was estimated at a monthly shipment of 25 ship tons of supplies for the duration of the deployment. With naval transports in short supply, this was not an insignificant task for the U.S. Navy to undertake.

I watched with interest as the presidential actions led to a detachment of U.S. Marines from the First Marine Brigade (Provisional) deploying to Iceland in early July of 1941, and I knew that I soon would be among the troops relieving them. The Army units that were scheduled to replace the Marines came from the 10th Infantry Regiment, the 5th Engineers, and the 46th Field Artillery Battalion, all from Fort Custer, Michigan; the 33rd Pursuit Squadron (P40s) and an Aircraft Engineer unit from Langley Air Base, Virginia; and the necessary service elements that were to remain in Iceland for the duration of the war. The initial U.S. Army deployment consisted of approximately 5,000 men—and I was among them.[5]

The U.S. Army presence in Iceland did not go unnoticed by the German Navy. Admiral Erich Raeder, in July 1941 complained that "the whole situation in the Atlantic has become more unfavorable for all our forces because of the occupation of Iceland and the increasing effect of United States support (of Britain)."[6]

NOTES

1. The German invasion plan for Iceland was code-named IKARUS. It was presented to Hitler on 2 June 1940, but never acted upon. The plan called for the German troops to enter Iceland at four points: Reykjavik, Hvalfjord, Akureyri, and Seydisfjord. It was anticipated that the occupation would be complete in four days.

2. The U.K. occupation of Iceland was code-named OPERATION FORK and commenced on 8 May 1940. The occupation was initiated without prior approval of the Icelandic government. Many of the U.K. troops deployed to Iceland were veterans of the Dunkirk evacuation and were considered to be among the best of the U.K. soldiers.

3. The Icelandic government, the Althing, had voted to allow the U.S. government to establish a base on Iceland on the following conditions: (1) the U.S. would respect Icelandic sovereignty; (2) the U.S. would leave Iceland at the close of the hostilities; and (3) the U.S. would provide a defense force at no cost to Iceland.

4. Extracted from "Documents on American Foreign Relations IV," pp. 354–358.

5. The short-term presence of the U.S. Marines in Iceland represents one of the rare land deployments of a U.S. Marine unit to serve in the European Theater during the Second World War. The U.S. Command was initially known as the Iceland Base Command and remained that until 30 July 1944 when it was incorporated into the East Defense Command.

6. Führer Conference, 1941 (Reporting Conferences of 1941).

Iceland Base Command

August 1941 to December 1941

Once the decision was made to place U.S. military forces in Iceland, things began to move quickly, though not without some controversy. When the First Marine Brigade (Provisional), under the command of Brigadier General John Marston, arrived on 7 July 1941, all was well. However, when it became known that the U.S. Army, as well as the Marines, would be deployed to Iceland, questions arose about whether a Marine or Army general would be the senior U.S. commander there. I watched the competitive military services at work! The question was bandied around the halls of Washington until 29 August 1941, when finally the Office of the Chief of Staff in the War Department sent a memo to Admiral Harold Stark, Chief of Naval Operations (CNO):

> I am of the opinion that the United States forces in Iceland should be under one commander, who should be given, to the extent legally possible full authority and responsibility. The Commander's authority should not be restricted to that contemplated in "Joint Action of the Army and the Navy for the Exercise of 'Unity of Command.'"
>
> In order to give the Commander of United States Forces in Iceland the authority legally possible over the combined forces, I propose that Marine forces in Iceland be detached for service with the Army. There is attached hereto a joint letter transmitting to the President a draft of an Executive Order which will accomplish the proposed detachment. Since the Army contingent will sail on or about September 5 it is very desirable that this matter be expedited.

The presidential executive order was signed, and the question of command was settled, but the selection of the actual commander remained. The Army now had to choose a general senior to the Marine general, Brigadier General Marston, who was already there. That ruled out Brigadier General Homer, who did not outrank General Marston, but the problem was quickly settled. The Army troops going to Iceland came predominately from the 5th Infantry Division commanded by Major General Charles H. Bonesteel—a well-respected third-generation West Point graduate (class of 1908), who had served with General Marshall and was currently the commanding general of the 5th Infantry Division at Fort Custer, Michigan. Without much debate, Major General Bonesteel was selected to be deployed as the senior U.S. commander in Iceland. General Homer was deployed to Iceland as the chief of staff to General Bonesteel. He was later promoted to the rank of major general and sent to the Panama Canal Zone. By coincidence, General Bonesteel's son, Captain Charles (Tick) Bonesteel, was also assigned to the Iceland Base Command. He was, like his father, a West Point graduate assigned to the Corps of Engineers. Tick and I became well acquainted during our time in Iceland, and our careers would cross again when we were both assigned to Europe.

Army Air Force elements soon followed the Marine's deployment. P-38 and P-39 units of the Army Air Corps with support elements were deployed in August of 1941, and finally Army troops arrived en masse on 16 September 1941 (all under the code name Project INDIGO). I was among the troops deployed in September. I would be the public affairs officer and assistant G-2. It was a challenging assignment in many ways. I not only was responsible for public affairs with the local population but also was charged with ensuring that our troops maintained high morale—and that was the real challenge. Iceland is not exactly a geographically friendly environment. Another assignment, and one that I found distasteful, was serving as the local Army counterintelligence officer, as I had at Fort Sheridan. This required soldiers to report on suspected subversive activity. Thankfully this initiative was soon judged counterproductive, and the U.S. Army canceled the program.

When I was notified of my new assignment, I was also given a short leave to spend with my family in Grand Rapids. By this time we had three young and vibrant children. It was a bittersweet visit, as I knew that it would be some time before I would be back. Although

I would miss her, I had no doubt about my wife, Grace, being able to cope with the situation; she was a very strong woman. It was just that like many departing fathers, I would be missing many of the formative years of my children. At my new assignment, temporarily at Fort Sheridan, I was greeted by a scene of sheer chaos. Regular Army troops selected for the Iceland Command were arriving without knowing where they would be going or what their duties would be. Arrangements had to be made with the Navy to maintain a supply line, which was no small task as transports were in critical supply. And perhaps most maddening was that, save for a few maps, the Army had no intelligence information on the nation it was about to inhabit—a sad demonstration of the dismal state of affairs in which isolationism had left the nation's armed forces. We scoured all elements of the government for their intelligence on Iceland but came up with limited information.

When we arrived at the Port of New York, from which we would ship to Iceland (our destination still unknown to the troops), General Bonesteel inquired as to the intelligence we had on our future base. The answer was "very little, beyond some general maps!" To fill the vacuum, the general sent me into the city, to one of the downtown Brentano's bookstores, to purchase whatever I could find that would provide some additional information. I bought a book called *Iceland*, by Vladimer Stephenson, and that was a major source of intelligence concerning Iceland—our future home away from home.

We sailed from New York to Iceland on U.S. Navy transports—the *Heywood*, the *William P. Brook*, the *Henry L. Lee*, and the *Republic*. Navy officials believed our passage would be safe, because the U.S. government was aware from intelligence sources that German U-boats were still under orders not to attack U.S. ships. But I remember hearing loud blasts from the sea as our destroyer escorts dropped depth charges all the way there.

Just before deployment from New York, I had received an additional duty—I had become a second aide-de-camp to General Bonesteel, which put me in regular contact with the commander. I well remember one moment of sheer panic during that trip. I was with the general in his quarters when the finance officer burst in, in a very worried state. When questioned by the general, he gave a response that sent chills up our spines. Why? When we left New York, there had been over a million dollars filling the safe in the hold, but now there was only about half that amount! The finance officer and the general could just see their military careers coming to inauspicious ends. Along with another officer, I was sent to count the money. Our results caused a sigh of relief. It seems that the rising and falling of the ship as it moved through the waters had compacted the money. On initial inspection, it appeared to be about half the original amount; but much to everyone's relief, our actual count proved that to be false.

The vessels that transported us to Iceland carried a second set of sealed orders that were not to be opened until we had disembarked and joined the U.S. Marines. Unsealing them as we were disembarking in Iceland, the officers of the Navy vessels discovered that they had little time to respond to their new deployment, so we were quickly left on our own. Piles of equipment, heaps of supplies, and masses of soldiers stood on the pier, the latter gazing at a land in sharp contrast to the one home they had just left behind. Iceland was formed by lava flows that spewed from the floor of the ocean and is blanketed with ice, mountains, and volcanoes but—because of the inhospitable ground covering—no trees. It is meteorologically uninviting, assailed by strong winds and rain, not to mention polar nights that in January can last as long as 21 hours and that in June and July are virtually nonexistent. This was the land our troops found themselves in, as they stood on the pier surrounded by their supplies.

The biggest loss was that the ships departing under their sealed orders had been carrying our fresh, perishable supplies, including meat. After we were disembarked, they had fulfilled their task—and their orders said to depart at that point, which they did, taking our fresh food supplies with them. Thus began the famous Spam diet.

We had not had time to build shelters or storage for the vast amount of supplies that arrived with us. They were just dumped on the docks, and we were left to our ingenuity. The situation was remedied with American know-how, as seen in the photographs in this section. By the end of our first year we had completely corrected the situation. The U.S. government, upon learning of our early misfortune with foodstuffs, decided to remedy it, and some months later sent us tons of fresh meat and vegetables. I actually got tired of eating beef in all of its various forms.

The Marines who preceded us had been fewer in number, and the facilities they had constructed did not begin to accommodate the needs of the Army forces that had just arrived. The challenges created

American troops arrive in Iceland. The deployment of U.S. military personnel to Iceland in September 1941 represented the first time U.S. forces entered the European theater since World War I. The troops were there at the request of the Icelandic government.

by forging an existence in a foreign land kept troop morale high initially. Huts had to be erected, lines of communications established, roads carved out of the barren Icelandic terrain, and storage areas established. The fact that we had been required to take seasoned military personnel worked to our advantage, as the enlisted troops just dug in and did their jobs, with no arguments or attitude problems. Draftees might have wondered why they were stationed in Iceland, since the United States had not officially entered the European war. Because the draft had just started in 1940, it was thought that draftees might not have the same deep commitment of experienced personnel, who had careers to think of and most of whom accepted their deployment unquestioningly.

We found the people of Iceland highly reserved and well educated. They were neither insulting nor aggressive toward their "welcomed occupiers." And they could soon see the improvements we were making in their roads and communications systems. Only once did I observe a competitive nature, and that was in the business of disposing of our latrine waste. It was a business highly sought, as the "honey buckets" with their waste contents were used to fertilize the vegetables, fruits, and other hothouse plants. It did not take long for our medical staff to issue an order forbidding the purchase of such items.

At no time during the deployment to Iceland were the American troops fed with food products from Iceland. The locals own supply was sparse, and we did not want to interfere with their food chain. As an officer, I could and did occasionally go into a local hotel for a dinner and was a little startled the first time I read the menu—the specialty of the house was pony meat! It made me grateful for Army beef again.

Iceland also gained a great deal in the deployment. In addition to the protection factor, logistically they also gained. Many roads were built by the U.S. Army—roads that did not exist at all prior to the deployment. Miles of telephone lines were installed, pipes were installed from the geysers to heat more of Reykjavik, and we built a huge airfield at Keflavik—it had to be greatly expanded to meet the U.S. Army needs and was left in place when we left.

My initial primary duty in Iceland was as public affairs officer (PAO) on the G-2 (intelligence) staff of the general staff—I also served as the assistant G-2. As we were not entirely welcome guests of the Icelandic government, this was challenging. Not only did I have to

Supply storage: September 1941 (TOP) *versus September 1942* (BOTTOM).

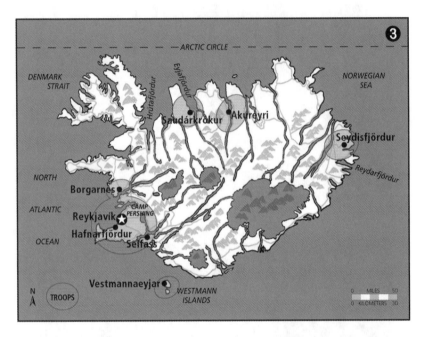

Deployment of U.S. troops in Iceland. The U.S. troops were deployed along similar lines of the U.K. forces. The U.S. Army Headquarters, Camp Pershing, was located just north of Reykjavik. The majority of the forces were deployed around Reykjavik, as that was the most populated area. Outposts were established at the entrances of the major fjords: that is, Seydisfjordur, Akureyri, Saudarkrokur, and the island of Vestmannaeyjar.

"calm the waters" with the local population, but also I had to placate the troops regarding their semi-isolation from the Icelandic people since they were not allowed to fraternize with the native population. My position as PAO made it important for me to understand the Icelandic people and to connect with the proper authorities in their government. I found both the citizens and the government to be taciturn, hardworking, and intensely patriotic about their sometimes-overlooked country. They were aware that U.S. forces were there to keep the country safe from the threat of a German takeover, and they accepted our presence quietly.

However, almost immediately after our arrival the Icelandic government put my duties as PAO to the test. We received a telephone call stating that the prime minister wished to meet with General Bonesteel, but no specific subject was given. The prime minister was concerned about the potential repeat of an incident in which four Marines raped an Icelandic woman. He proposed a simple solution. Certain ladies in Iceland had "tarnished" reputations, he said, and they could be installed in a government-run brothel for the explicit use of U.S. Army personnel. No sooner had he said this than General Bonesteel, straight-laced West Pointer that he was, reacted with a resounding "No!" That was the end of the proposal. Fortunately, the issue would not be a major concern during the Army's stay.

While the troops accepted their deployment and went about their jobs, as the days began to settle down into a normal routine, morale did become a problem. The foul weather in Iceland—combined with the extended periods of night and day, combined with the fact that troops were restricted to the bases and had little interaction with the local population—did take its toll. One has only to stroll through the cemeteries in Iceland to see the names of U.S. Army soldiers who were killed by accident or committed suicide during those early days of the occupation.

As a former newspaperman, I pondered how to relieve their homesickness and, in some cases, despair. I had started a weekly newspaper at Fort Sheridan and thought that would be an excellent idea for the troops in Iceland, too. Prior to landing, I discussed it with our commander, who heartily agreed. The paper, which replaced the previous publication, the *Bugle* (which had been started by the Army Air Corps crew in Iceland), described events happening both back in the United States and right there among our own troops. The newspaper was called the *White Falcon* (the national bird of Iceland), and it was an immediate success, not only with the soldiers but among the local population as well. The paper was published on a weekly basis for as long as American troops remained in Iceland. (The *White Falcon* is still published by the Iceland Defense Force Staff—a U.S. forces unit based in Iceland.)

The first edition of the newspaper, published on 27 September 1941, carried a front-page article regarding the new United States/ British military cooperation on Iceland. The British were generally pleased to have us there, and the article described the beginnings of the World War II military cooperation between the two countries. This initial edition did not carry much stateside news or, more importantly to the troops, the sports or comics. Realizing this, I got in touch with some of my newspaper friends in the States, and before long we were able to increase our national news, include the national sports results, and even have a full page of comics. The troops loved it.

For that first edition I had an artist prepare a drawing showing the Americans and the British greeting one another with handshakes. It was picked up by the *New York Times* and shown on their page one of the overseas edition, which was very pleasing to General Bonesteel as his picture was on page one. It also appeared in the stateside edition of the *New York Times,* for 8 November 1941, page 7, section one.

The masthead of the paper contained the names of the editorial staff: managing editor, Pfc. Edward Murray Jr,; news editor, Pfc. Peter T. Macy; and circulation editor, Donald A. Sidenberg. It also stated, "This paper has been passed by the censor and may be mailed home for one cent," which was a big morale booster for the troops. Their families could now get a glimpse into their lives in Iceland. While this service sounded nice, it was almost impossible to meet the requirements for mailing, and few succeeded in getting to the States. Then once the war began, the commanding general ordered that the *White Falcon* could no longer be sent to the families at home.

When I look back on those early editions, they really bring back how naive and complacent we were before the 7th of December and how incensed we became after the attack on Pearl Harbor. The two front pages shown clearly demonstrate this. The first, dated 6 December 1941, has a front-page article about a "Nifty Nissan" hut competition being held for our forces in Iceland, and while it contains war news, there is no apparent threat to the U.S. The second, dated one week later, 13 December 1941, has a completely different

THE WHITE FALCON

No. 1. Reykjavik, Iceland, Saturday, Sept. 27th 1941. Price: 3 cents (20 aurar)

Troops Move Into Camps.

Well done, my lads.

It isn't often a sergeant speaks to his men in such terms, but the expression is most appropriate in the case of soldiers, who worked day and night in getting equipment off boats and into new camp sites.

Fact that the unloading of equipment had been given thorough study was evidenced by the manner in which members of the command progressed. A steady stream of trucks pounded the roads between camps and unloading point for eight days and nights, and on the ninth day, Wednesday, headquarters were functioning at all stations.

The transition was accomplished with few mishaps, the main difficulty being breakdown of vehicles, either by accident or mechanical defects.

TAPS

The old order giveth the way to the new and so the American Army Bugle bows out making way for The White Falcon. We have enjoyed putting out the old paper but know that this new addition to the newssheets in Iceland will be bigger and we hope better than our earliest effort. The Falcon, by way of explanation of our new title, is the national bird of the Icelandic people and in tribute to them we are proud that they allow us to use this symbol in conjunction with our American eagle.

Walsh Asks Greer Log

WASHINGTON. — Chairman Walsh of the Senate Naval Committee requested Naval Secretary Frank Knox Friday to produce the official log of the Destroyer Greer, publicly. Especially for the entire day of its encounter with a German submarine off Iceland. This to let the public know just what had happened. Isolationist Senators claimed that the Greer fired first at the German submarine.

BRITISH, U.S. GENERAL in EXCHANGE of LETTERS

An exchange of letters between the commanding generals of the British forces and the American army was announced today. A reprint of the letters follows:

19th September, 1941.

Major-General C. H. Bonesteel.
Commanding U.S. Forces in Iceland.

On my own behalf and that of the British Forces in Iceland, may I extend to you and to the U. S. Army about to land a most hearty welcome to Iceland.

During recent weeks the British Forces have deeply appreciated the privilege of working in the closest cooperation with their friends the U. S. Marines and U. S. Airforce in the defense of this vital strategic point. Now all are looking forward to the same honour with the U. S. Army.

All feel the importance of the historic fact of the troops of the two great democracies standing here shoulder to shoulder in the fight for freedom against Nazidom, and as a result enjoying the feeling of absolute confidence in final victory.

(Signed) H. O. CURTIS.
Major-General,
Commanding British Forces in Iceland.

HEADQUARTERS ICELAND BASE COMMAND.

Reykjavik, Iceland.

20th September, 1941.

Major General H. O. Curtis, C.B., D.S.O., M.C.

It is with distinct soldierly pride and appreciation that I hasten to acknowledge your most cordial letter of welcome to me and to the latest American addition to the common defense of this island.

Such a gesture of comradeship and good will from veterans who have blazed the trail of Icelandic defense is a spur to our finest effort.

I am indeed happy and proud to be associated with the splendid soldiers of His Majesty's Forces in the protection of this northern outpost, and I assure you that this feeling is shared by every member of the American Forces.

Your gracious message is being published to my entire command.

C. H. BONESTEEL.
Major General, U.S. Army,
Commanding.

DODGERS WIN

WORLD SERIES TO START ON WEDNESDAY

By taking both ends of a double header on Thursday, the Dodgers won the right to raise the first pennant flag in 21 years over Ebbets Field and to settle the long dispute between the ardent Flatbush fans and the Bronxites as to their chances of Spirit against long hitting.

Seldom more than three games away from the Scrappy Cards the Durocher men entered the final stretch this week, with a slim lead. This margin was slashed on Sunday, when the Redbirds beat the Cubs 6—5 and 7—0, while the Brooks split a twin bill with the lowly Phils, taking the first game 8 to 3 and dropping the second 6—3.

The Dodgers regained a half a game of their precious lead on Monday by blanking the Phils 5—0 while the Cards were idle.

The Cards muffed their big chance to catch the idle Brooks

(Continued on page 4.)

Photo by U.S. Army Air Corps.
MAJOR-GENERAL
C. H. BONESTEEL,
commanding officer of the Iceland Base Command shown with Lt. Col. R. M. Morris, commanding officer of the Air Corps Unit upon the former's arrival.

First issue of the White Falcon, *a newspaper for troops in Iceland, dated 27 September 1941, as shown in the* New York Times, *8 November 1941. The white falcon is the national bird of Iceland.*

mood. We are now at war! It displays cartoon images of both Hitler and Mussolini predominately on the front page and speaks of the first U.S. hero, a pilot by the name of Colin Kelly.[1] We were no longer a shadow element—we were at war.

The next issue to arise was that while the American presence in Iceland was now known, we, as individuals could tell no one back in the States where we were stationed, especially family members. All they had was an APO address, with no country location, and, in return, all letters going out of Iceland were heavily censured to delete all references to the location of the troops. To alleviate the problem, as morale was getting very low, I requested permission to create and publish a short book, titled *The American Forces in Iceland*. I proposed to have pictures of facilities and activities, without giving the name of any individual stationed there, beyond Major General Charles H. Bonesteel and his staff officers—since it had become public knowledge that he headed a task force in Iceland.

General Bonesteel initially said "no," as he was concerned about a lack of funding to support the publication. When I told him that we could sell it in the PX, and that I would put up the initial money to get it published, he came around. That way, every GI could send it home with no breach of security, and his family would have an idea of where he was and what he was doing. The book was published in November of 1941, after a front-page announcement in the 22 November 1941 edition of the *White Falcon*.

It was an instant success—selling out the first edition of 500 copies in only three days. Soldiers found that the mailing envelopes included with each copy provided an easy way to send family members a clue as to their location without any major breaches of military security taking place.

The book served another purpose as well—that of counterpoint to the newspaper pictures and other stories then coming out of Iceland. Three very capable newsmen reporting from Iceland—Drew Pearson of the Associated Press, Phil Auldt of the United Press, and William Wade of the International News Service— had been sending out descriptions of the rudimentary huts soldiers lived in, the rutted roads they traveled on, and the barren landscapes they woke up to each morning. Officers feared that such scenes would dissuade young men from enlisting in the service. These public affairs officers—and the book itself—worked to put a positive, adventuresome spin on the conditions troops lived and worked in throughout their time in Iceland.

THE WHITE FALCON

PUBLISHED FOR AMERICAN FORCES IN ICELAND

Vol. 1, No. 11.   Reykjavik, Iceland, Saturday, Dec. 6, 1941.   Price: 3 cents (20 aurar)

News Roundup

RUSSIAN FRONT

Kuibishev. The city of Taganrog is believed to be in Russian hands again, Soviet sources said as a result of the Red Army counter offensive smashing the Germans back from Rostov over a 100 mile road toward Mariupol, Taganrog, on the Sea of Azov, lies 40 miles west of Rostov, which the Russians recaptured last Saturday.

Berlin. German armored forces were officially reported driving closer to Moscow and a military spokesman said that Axis troops had taken up a new and stronger defense line against the Red army attacks in the Rostov area. The Russian attacks in the south appeared to be aided by strong bombing attacks.

LIBYAN FRONT

London. British reinforcements fought to regain the initiative on the main Libyan battlefield but for the time being at least German armored units dominated the vital front south of Tobruk. Authorized sources said the vague communiques issued by General headquarters at Cairo indicated the battle continued very fluid but that Axis forces which recaptured Sidi Rezegh still maintained control of the corridor leading to Tobruk.

Earlier a British thrust had reached the Cyrenaican coast east of Benghazi, but late developments of the week would indicate this thrust may be surrounded.

Berlin. A high command communique said that Axis forces had encircled the bulk of a New Zealand division southeast of Tobruk on the Adem front and part of its personnel had been destroyed and part taken prisoner.

FAR EAST

Washington.—Informed quarters said withdrawal of Japanese

(Continued on page 8).

A winner? We doubt it, but at least any nude curtains, a washstand, wires for drying clothes and a few other innovations, which could form a part of a winning suggestion in the "Nifty Nissen" contest conducted by The White Falcon.

VICHY APPROVES NAZI OCCUPATION OF NORTH AFRICA

London. According to reports reaching here the Franco-German pact signed this week at Florence, by Air Marshal Goering and Premier Petain, will permit German occupation of North Africa.

Occupation of French West Africa was not arranged, and observers believed that this move was avoided to prevent provocation of the United States.

Spanish observers admitted that arrangements had been made a year ago for passage of German troops through Spain and Spanish Morocco. It was believed that this route would be used by the Germans in occupying the French Colonies. Large scale troop movements have been made recently, westward from Alsace to the Spanish border.

Final arrangements for Franco-Spanish defense of West Africa were settled in Berlin, when representatives of the Governments were there to sign the Anti-Comintern Pact.

The Vichy capitulation in North Africa is expected to give the Germans an enormously better position in the Libyan campaign.

HEAVY TANK PRODUCTION

Washington. The War Department announced Friday that the first heavy tank to be manufactured in the United States will be demonstrated December 8th at the Baldwin Locomotive works. It is a 55 ton tank of 1,500 horsepower.

The announcement said that everything was ready for mass production.

The importance of heavy tank production is illustrated by the fact that only American light tanks have been used in the Libyan campaign, the announcer said.

Christmas Issue

The White Falcon plans a special Christmas edition, to be published Christmas week. The editor desires that every unit be represented in this big issue.

Deadline for the Christmas copy is December 10.

Falcon Sponsors Hut Contest: 100 kr. Prize

The White Falcon, starting next Monday, will sponsor a "Nifty Nissen" contest in which 100 krónur is to be awarded for original ideas on improving interior of huts.

Prizes will be 60 krónur for first place; 30 krónur for second, and 10 krónur for third. All entries must be in the Contest Editor, The White Falcon, Camp Pershing, not later than January 5th, 1942.

Any member of the American Force is eligible to participate and must write his suggestion in not more than 100 words; such entries may be submitted any time between next Monday and the deadline, January 5th. Judges for the contest will be Captain Edwin Machen, of the personnel section; Tech Sergeant Noble Hill, plans and training section, and a representative of The White Falcon.

"Thils originality will be most factor in deciding the winner, entries are cautioned that their suggestions must be practical and already in use. Once the suggestion appears most favored by the judges a trip will be made to the winner's hut where a first hand view may be afforded. Pictures also will be published in The White Falcon on the three winners and description of their "Nifty Nissens".

THE WHITE FALCON

PUBLISHED FOR AMERICAN FORCES IN ICELAND

Vol. I, No. 12.   Reykjavik, Iceland, Saturday, Dec. 13, 1941.   Price: 3 cents (20 aurar)

MARINES STILL HOLDING WAKE

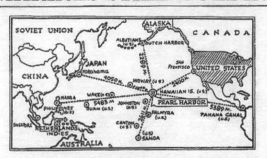

The waters of the Pacific, dotted with islands, has become the main theater of operations for the American and British forces in that area. The above map shows key points of the present conflict.

U.S. LASHES AT AXIS

The United States in all her armed and economic might lashed out at the axis this week. In the Pacific the American and British navies were recovering from the surprise of the Japanese attack, and were blasting away at the Japanese fleet.

In Washington, Americans faced complete mobilization of the world's greatest production to assure victory.

A giant victory campaign contemplating expenditure of $150,000,000,000 per year for armament was under way.

These were the major events which plunged the U. S. into total war.

Sunday Japanese naval and air forces attacked Pearl Harbor, Manila, Malaya, Guam and Wake Island and the Imperial Japanese government announced it was at war with the United States and Great Britain. Monday morning Great Britain declared war on Japan. Monday afternoon President Roosevelt asked Congress for

a declaration of war on Japan and a resolution was passed in Congress. Before the weeks end 17 nations had declared war on Japan.

Thursday morning Adolf Hitler issued a scathing denunciation of President Roosevelt, accusing him of "Warmongering", saying "The blood of Europe is on his hands" .... that he had been responsible for the prolongation of the war in Europe. Accusing Roosevelt of ordering the U.S. Navy to fire upon German submarines and ships in violation of inter-

national law. He said, "I am not insulted by Mr. Roosevelts remarks about me, because I believe that Mr. Roosevelt like Mr. Wilson is insane. Germany declared war on the United States.

That same Thursday morning Benito Mussolini went out onto the Pallazzio Venetia and announced Italy's declaration of war on the U.S. Democracy, he said, would be erased from the earth.

The Congress of the United States received a short terse message from President Roosevelt and within thirty six minutes had declares war on both Germany and Italy.

For a full chronology of the events of the week see pages four and five.

First American Hero is Dead

British Attack

To Register Men From 18 to 65

Washington — President Roosevelt, in his Friday press conference gave special commendation to the gallant force of Marines defending Wake Island. They were very highly praised for their valiant stand against repeated Japanese attacks.

The small garrison has been under constant siege since Sunday and is still holding out. Yesterday the War Department announced that they had destroyed a Japanese light cruiser and a destroyer. This report was confirmed in Tokyo. It is believed the Japanese warships were downed by fire of three and five inch anti aircraft guns.

Washington, America's first hero of the new war has been killed in action. He is Captain Colin Kelly of the United States Navy, who is credited with dropping the bomb which destroyed the Japanese battleship Haruna Thursday. Another Japanese battleship of the Kongo class was badly damaged and believed destroyed Friday.

London. — A British offer of the entire output of three Canadian munition plants for one month was revealed here by Prime Minister Churchill and Lord Beaverbrook.

(Continued on page 8).

War message	P. 7
War declaration	P. 7
Roosevelt report	P. 7
War events	Pp. 4, 5, 6

Front page of the White Falcon, *13 December 1941.*

THE WHITE FALCON

PUBLISHED FOR AMERICAN FORCES IN ICELAND

Vol. 1, No. 9.   Reykjavik, Iceland, Saturday, Nov. 22, 1941.   Price: 3 cents (20 aurar)

News Roundup

WASHINGTON. Secretary of Navy Knox opined that American ships would be on their way to ports of belligerent nations by next Monday. This forecast was made after President Roosevelt signed the bill permitting such action last Monday. Brother cabinet member, Cordell Hull held two conferences with Japan's clever diplomat Kurusu. At the last meeting on Thursday the talk lasted for an hour and it was believed Kurusu had received new instructions from his country.

PITTSBURGH. Coal strikes seemed no nearer conclusion despite the fact President Roosevelt sent workers and mine owners identical letters pointing out that the nation's security depended on settlement of the strike. Upon receipt of the letter mine owners agreed to the President's course. John L. Lewis, however, is holding up his reply until today.

LONDON. General Sir John Dill has been replaced as commander-in-chief of the British army by General Sir Alan Brooke.

VICHY. Removal of General Weygand as commander in North Africa was seen by the democracies as further signs of German pressure. Result of this latest move was believed by many in U. S. as indication American economic assistance to France would be put aside.

MOSCOW. The battle for Moscow has flared up again in the midst of heavy snowfall and bitter cold. Elsewhere on the Russian front the Nazis have started a big drive for Rostow. Sebastopol remains the only key position in the Crimea not taken by the Germans.

BERLIN. The Germans claim progress in their battle of Russia and say they have captured 10,000 prisoners. They failed to mention names.

Commends Two Soldiers For Act During Fire

Public commendation was given this week to two soldiers, both members of the ordnance, who without regard for their own safety removed valuable equipment from a burning tent.

The men, Pvts. John C. Hopkins and Quinton Hale, were awakened at 2 o'clock in the morning of November 9th by a fire in the guard tent at the ordnance depot and, despite the fact great personal risk was involved, managed to remove several boxes containing pistols and machine guns.

During this act both men received burns, mostly on the hands, but continued their task until all property was safely removed.

For their deed a personal letter written by Major General Charles H. Bonesteel, commanding general of the army forces in Iceland, was given the soldiers.

Japs Prepare If United States Parlay Fails

Tokyo. Japanese observers agree the Diet has completed its task of preparing for the worse eventuality if the U.S. Japanese negotiations fail.

The Diet approved thirteen bills the most important of which was the appropriation of 800,000,000 yen for extraordinary military expenditures.

New information chief Hori declined to comment Friday afternoon on a Shanghai report that Kurusu had offered to guarantee Japanese neutrality in the European conflict and guarantee East asian territorial integrity drop her southward push —in exchange for relaxation of the economic blockade and United States good offices toward a Sino-Japanese settlement. He said he was refraining from statement until the proper time.

DOUG FAIRBANKS JR. HERE WITH NAVY

REYKJAVIK. Douglas Fairbanks Jr., hero of scores of action movies willingly admitted he "was really scared" during weeks long service on active duty as Lieutenant Junior Grade in the U. S. Navy aboard a destroyer on convoy duty in the North Atlantic.

Nattily dressed in a regulation naval blue and gold uniform and greatcoat, his blonde mustaches still as trim as when he was in films Fairbanks talked enthusiastically of his experiences. He visited Reykjavik for the first time on leave from the battleship where he was recently transferred for the duration of three months active tour of duty before returning to the service of his State department. He found Reykjavik "interesting, but slightly quiet."

The film star admitted with sheepish grin that he suffered considerably from seasickness several times aboard the rolling destroyer but kept going.

"We rolled fifty seven degrees once then back to fifty six degrees the other side. We were forced to walk on the bulkheads instead of the deck, and were hardly able to go to our bunks at all. Several men suffered injuries. I had a leg scraped slightly bouncing around in a heavy sea. The destroyer experience was exciting. I am certainly glad I had it. I have a great admiration for the men who serve regularly but I am perfectly content to serve the rest of my duty aboard a battleship."

At coffee hour at the Borg he met a beautiful Icelandic girl, asked her what she thought of American Naval officers. She replied in Icelandic "I think they are very beautiful". He failed to understand, looked blank, she added in English the comment typical the world over "You look just like your pictures", he grinned.

BOOKLET TO BE PUBLISHED ON U.S. TROOPS HERE

An illustrated booklet, "The American Forces in Iceland", depicting the arrival and subsequent activities of American forces in this northern Atlantic outpost is being published next week for the American troops. Copies will be made available the first week in December.

Sponsored by the White Falcon, the booklet will contain more than a score of pictures on activities of American forces and an almost equal number of scenic photographs on Iceland. Accompanying each picture will be an explanatory paragraph.

Besides the illustrations the booklet will devote seven full pages of written matter in explanation of our activities and give a historical background of Iceland.

The number of copies to be distributed will be definitely limited and since no attempt is made to make large profits it will sell for approximately two krónur.

Published timely, so as to make an ideal Christmas souvenir, the booklet is intended to be of special interest to friends and relatives in the United States. All branches of the American forces are given representation in the publication.

Althing Closes

Reykjavik. The Althing, after a turbulent week which saw the Jonasson government begin its third term in office, adjourned Friday noon. The next session will begin February 15.

The White Falcon, *announcement of booklet to be published about troops in Iceland, 22 November 1941.*

The first book, *The American Forces in Iceland*, had to be very discreet and not show faces of any of the American troops—we were still an unknown unit. However, once the United States entered the war, that changed, and our second book on Iceland could include photographs of many of the troops. The wraps were off, and we had become a legitimate U.S. Army unit. I titled the second book, *Armed Guardians: One Year in Iceland*, and published it in November 1942. As with the first, it was an instant best seller. I was the unknown author of two best sellers!

Recreation was always a problem for the troops; they were confined to the post in a rather depressing climate. To pass the time, I began to play a card game I had been taught by my grandfather—the game of cribbage. And since it was originally a British game, it was only natural that my British counterpart decided to teach me the "finer points" of the game. I decided that a U.S./U.K. cribbage tournament, open to all American and British personnel, would be a great boost to morale. It was organized, and as it progressed, the scores were posted on a big wall in the recreational area. The final outcome of the tournament was a bit "dicey," as I ended up beating General Bonesteel, as well as my British tutor. I still, to this day, occasionally play cribbage with my wife using the cribbage board made by my grandfather.

I served on many court-martial boards during my time in Iceland, and two cases remain particularly vivid. The first was for desertion. A soldier got very homesick and wanted to go home—which was only possible by desertion. Desperate to accomplish this, he hid on a freighter that made a port call in Iceland. He was caught and tried by a general court-martial and was found guilty. As it was considered wartime, the maximum sentence possible was the death penalty. Some of the members on the board voted for a sentence of death, but I could not and would not. Finally the man was sentenced to life in prison. (At that time, the War Department was lenient, and I am sure his sentence was commuted later.)

The second involved a murder. An officer was found dead in his quarters with a bullet in his head. The case was investigated, and finally the investigators came to tell me that they had solved the case. It turned out that a soldier, suffering from alcoholism, was in desperate need of a drink. None was available, but he knew that officers were allowed to keep whiskey in their rooms—hence the murder. When I asked the investigators how they solved the case, they said by

THE AMERICAN FORCES
IN ICELAND

Cover of The American Forces in Iceland, *published in November 1941. From its introduction: "This booklet has been published for a two-fold purpose. First, it gives the American forces in Iceland a pictorial history of their early days in the northern Atlantic outpost; and secondly, it is printed before Christmas so as to reach those relatives and friends back home whose help and confidence gives us our will and courage."*

ARMED GUARDIANS

ONE YEAR IN
ICELAND

ARMED GUARDIANS
ONE YEAR IN ICELAND

PREPARED BY G-2 SECTION,
ICELAND BASE COMMAND

FÉLAGSPRENTSMIDJAN — NOVEMBER, 1942 — REYKJAVIK, ICELAND

Cover and title page of Armed Guardians: One Year in Iceland, *published in November 1942. This book is a testimonial to the efficiency of the American troops in Iceland.*

a confession. However, when pressed, they told me that the statement was obtained by putting a microphone in a confessional in the chapel, where the man had confessed to his priest. The trial did go on, and the man was found guilty, but the investigator who placed the microphone in the confessional was sent back to the States—we would not have him in Iceland. During the penalty phase I held out against the death penalty for the man due to extenuating circumstances, and he was subsequently sentenced to life in prison.

With the additional duty of being the assistant G-2, I became involved in the intelligence activities of the command. Even prior to our departure for Iceland, General Homer had told our G-2 section to "learn all we can from the British, but tell them nothing, if possible." I followed these instructions and did, in fact, learn a great deal about how to run an intelligence operation from my U.K. colleagues. I made a conscious effort to establish a close working relationship with my British counterpart, Commander Hugh Simpson of the Royal British Navy. It was under this tutelage that I learned the true depths of intelligence. It would prove of great value in my later Army career.

In my collaboration with British intelligence, specific events of 1940 were often relayed to me as an example of the lack of appreciation by senior officials for good intelligence. At that time, the Icelandic U.K. element had been aware of the British naval efforts to evacuate British troops from Norway, along with the king of Norway and about 700 of that country's senior officials. The U.K. Icelandic command detected and reported to the admiralty the presence of German battle cruisers, the *Schornhorst* and the *Gneisau* in their observation area off the coast of Norway, at the exact time the U.K. ships were undertaking the evacuation process. This information had also been reported to the admiralty by Bletchley Park, based on reading the German naval codes. No action was taken, although the U.K. aircraft carrier, the *Glorious*, in the same area as the German vessels, was believed by the U.K. to be carrying the Norwegian delegation. The *Glorious* was sunk with a major loss of life. The Norwegian delegation was actually on the HMS *Devonshire* where crew members heard the *Glorious* SOS but would not repeat it for security reasons. In fact, the *Glorious* evacuees were all British military personnel. In all, 1,451 British military men were lost with the sinking of the *Glorious* and her two destroyer escorts, the *Acosta* and the *Ardent*. Nothing about the event was reported in the press at the time. This tragedy may well have been averted if the intelligence data had been used. I wish I could report a lesson learned, but, unfortunately, it is a lesson we still learn over and over again.

I was soon to learn of another Norwegian effort in Iceland that would later impact Allied plans. In late 1940 Norwegian volunteers formed what became known as the Norwegian Company Iceland. The group worked with the U.K. and later the American troops, training them for winter warfare. On occasion they volunteered for missions back to Norway. Their presence was later deliberately made known, when they became an element of FORTITUDE NORTH, the deception plan focusing on an invasion of Norway at the same time as the Pais de Calais in France. That plan worked, as Hitler ordered 18 German divisions to be kept in Scandinavia to prevent an invasion. Some of the divisions remained there as late as spring 1945.

In the fall of 1941, 17 October to be exact, shortly after our arrival in Iceland, the German navy torpedoed a U.S. Navy destroyer, DD-432, the USS *Kearney*. The ship, badly damaged, managed to limp toward Iceland lashed to the side of another destroyer. I was party to the rescue force sent to render assistance. Fearing that German submarines were lurking nearby, we asked local Icelandic fisherman for transport to evacuate the wounded from the ship. We knew the Germans would not attack Icelandic craft. Our approach to the *Kearney* was not easily forgotten. The bow and the stern were intact, but the entire center section was missing—just a gaping hole remained. It was an amazing sight. The attack had consisted of the firing of two torpedoes. The first torpedo fired hit the *Kearney* and created the hole, the second torpedo fired had in fact gone cleanly through the newly created hole causing no further damage. The USS *Kearney* was a 1,650-ton destroyer launched in 1940. Her captain was A. L. Davis. In the attack, 11 men were killed and 24 were wounded. By early 1941 the ship had been repaired in Iceland by the U.S. Navy repair ship, the *Vulcan*, and returned to duty.

I had to ensure that the only reporting of the incident was by the commanding general to the War Department and that none of the news about the *Kearney* was reported to U.S. newspapers by the correspondents assigned in Iceland. We succeeded, because they were stationed in Reykjavik, which was far removed from the hub of the action. Any public reporting of the event could have been misconstrued as an act of war, thereby bringing the U.S. into the European conflict.

The torpedoing of the *Kearney* was followed on 31 October by another submarine attack on a U.S. destroyer. This time the ship was

46

The USS Kearney, *with the hole in her side clearly visible and lashed to another U.S. destroyer, arrives in Iceland for repair.*

the DD-245, the *Reuben James*, sunk about 600 miles off the coast of Iceland. We had speculated that the attack on the *Kearney* might have been in error, but the *Reuben James* had all the markings of a deliberate hit. The *Reuben James* lost 115 crew members, and only 45 survived. The survivors were rescued by the USS *Niblack*, herself a survivor of a U-boat attack. As a result of the *Reuben James* attack, Congress voted to amend the Neutrality Act with two conditions. The first permitted arming of American merchantmen, and the second abolished the restriction that denied European waters to American shipping. The U.S. Navy could now escort ships approved for use in the Lend-Lease Act. The war was getting closer.

It has never been determined whether the attack on the *Kearney* was deliberate or merely a case of mistaken identity. However, the torpedoing of the *Reuben James* a few weeks later left no doubt that Germany maintained hostile intentions toward the United States. The ship, a destroyer, had departed from Newfoundland on 23 October to escort a British convoy across the Atlantic and had been torpedoed by the German submarine U-552 about 600 miles off the coast of Iceland. President Roosevelt protested both attacks, but the German government refused to apologize, saying only that "anybody walking along the railroad track should not be surprised if he gets run over by an express train." The torpedoing of the *Reuben James* was thus considered to be the first hostile sinking of a U.S. Navy vessel in World War II, and it so enraged the American government that officials ordered on-sight attacks on any ship making aggressive overtures toward the United States. That marked America's first tentative, hesitant step toward immersion in the international conflict then raging across Europe.

U.S. Navy ships were not our only concern in Iceland. We were also using aircraft—both fighters and reconnaissance planes. Prior to the entry of the United States into the war, the fighters had little to do beyond training; however, the reconnaissance planes were employed constantly. Most were L5 light aircraft, which flew unarmed off the coast of Iceland, a dangerous mission due to the strong winds. I distinctly remember one sad event regarding a specific L5 plane. It was a very windy day, as it can be in Iceland, and the L5 was returning to base from a reconnaissance mission. The pilot tried to come in for a landing in one direction, but the wind was too strong, and he could not land. He then tried in another direction, but again the wind was too strong for the light plane to land, and finally, as we all stood in the airport, we watched as the small aircraft was blown out to sea and lost. Sadly, the pilot became another unheralded hero.

Our U.S. forces stationed in Iceland in the fall of 1941 were quite unprepared for a major attack. To the home front, we may have looked like the "forward vanguard" defending the shores of America, but in reality we were merely a shadow force. The troops were equipped with leftover World War I tin helmets and the same spats on their legs that had been worn by the likes of Sergeant York. They looked like a bunch of extras from a Hollywood film of the Great War.

Strategic plans for how our troops would function in the event of an attack by the Germans were limited, particularly considering we would have to coordinate command with the U.K. troops who remained in the area. We therefore spent a great deal of time exercising and trying to ascertain possible invasion routes and tactics. The lack of trees made defensive positions decidedly more difficult, and the unpredictable weather wreaked havoc with range schedules and bullet trajectories. Yet we knew these factors would not stop the Germans, and so our soldiers marched on, selecting artillery placements, establishing supply routes, and committing themselves body and soul in the defense of democracy, should such a need arise.

I had never seen the exact details of Germany's invasion plans for Iceland (Project IKARUS). All of our exercises were based on assumptions about where they would hit, and those places were limited due to the area's rugged geography. We were on particular alert when the German battleship the *Bismarck* was ready for action, accompanied by the battle cruisers *Schornhorst* and *Gneisau*, along with ancillary forces. Would they steam toward Iceland?

We often exercised with the British. On one occasion, it had been quite an active skirmish until 10 o'clock in the morning, when there was suddenly a complete silence over all the area of the British troops. When I arrived there I saw why—it was teatime; they had stopped for their "spot of tea." Our troops were deployed in much the same locations as the British had been. These positions were very isolated and inaccessible—not an easy duty station.

NOTE

1. Captain Colin Kelly was a B-17 pilot in the Pacific Theater. On 10 December 1941 his bomber damaged the Japanese cruiser the *Ashegara*. On the return mission his plane was hit by Japanese fighter fire. He stayed at the controls in order to allow his men to parachute into safety. He went down with the plane.

The United States Enters War in Europe

December 1941 to August 1943

On 7 December 1941 the mission of the United States Army in Iceland changed dramatically, as did the mission of U.S. forces everywhere. We watched as our government declared war on Japan on 9 December and, subsequently, as the German and Italian governments declared war on the United States on 11 December. We were now a legal military force at war.

Our forces in Iceland, the remaining Marines and the best the Army had at that time, assumed their role as the forward vanguard, the leading edge of the U.S. military presence in the European Theater as envisaged by General Marshall. The remaining Marines still present in Iceland were soon returned to the United States to be deployed with regular Marine units destined for duty in the Far East.[1] We of the Army were unsure of our future role, but we did know what our current mission dictated: to continue our defense of Iceland.

We had been regarded as peacekeepers, armed forces who drilled and prepared for attack but who trusted that the need for use of our weapons in combat would never materialize. Now we were the first thrust of American military presence in Europe, and we were engaged in a war against very real enemies. What our specific role in that war would be, we did not know, but we recognized the importance of our continued defense of this island nation, and we vowed that our vigilance in ensuring the protection would not wane.

This was because Iceland was a strategic location between Europe and North America and was considered valuable by Allies and Axis powers alike. American convoys were relying on Allied forces in Iceland to protect them as they crossed the North Atlantic. And American intelligence personnel in Iceland found themselves faced with the important task of intelligence gathering against German military forces in the nearby Scandinavian countries—particularly Norway,

51

which Germany had occupied in 1940. It was imperative that our vigilance remain steadfast, that we ensure that these activities were not threatened by possible German encroachment. We were acutely aware that the tie between Iceland and Germany was very strong, which made our intelligence-gathering efforts that much more difficult.

Almost immediately, on acceleration of war, the frequency of convoys crossing the North Atlantic increased substantially, and the Icelandic force became involved in both the air and the naval aspects of protecting those armadas. We became very aware of the bravery of those merchant marine ships.

While Iceland was isolated from the main European military arena, we were not infrequently reminded of its strategic location and potential value to the Allies, as well as to the Axis powers. As the armadas increased in frequency in the North Atlantic, we felt the value of having a U.S. contingent this close to Europe.

One of our first reminders of that occurred in the spring of 1942, when Soviet Foreign Minister Vyacheslav Molotov stopped in Iceland for several days on his way to Washington for discussions with President Roosevelt. During that time, being an ally, he was shown the airfields used by our fighters and bombers and other military strategic points, such as the fjords and the rendezvous points for the convoys on their way to resupply the USSR.

It is interesting to note that, prior to this visit, the USSR had no interest in Iceland, but after Molotov's visit, their interest increased. Almost immediately after the U.S. entered the war in Europe, the Soviet Union dispatched a large delegation and opened diplomatic relations with the Icelandic government. Molotov was quick to realize both the military and economic potential of a relationship with Iceland. The critical shipment of arms and supplies to the USSR from America depended on maintaining Iceland on the Allied side.

One evening after dinner, I remember I was sitting in the Officers' Club by the fireplace with a small group of Americans and one of the members of the Molotov party. We began an open discussion, and the Russian invited us to question him about the Soviet Union. We asked about the Communist Party campaign against organized religion, which he said was being conducted as a means of appropriating land from the considerable holdings of the church; about whether that nation maintained a need for better control of agricultural productivity; about Soviet purges of Tsarist supporters, which our sources said were meant to prevent the latter from mounting a counterrevolution; about why the Soviet Union had established a nonaggression pact with Hitler in 1939, deemed necessary if the Communists were to maintain their autonomy in the face of a potential German onslaught; and about many other issues. All of our questions were answered with what we felt were honest, albeit party line, responses.

We, of course, were most interested in learning how the war was progressing against the Germans and whatever we could discern about their military tactics and operations. Our Russian guest seemed somewhat reluctant to discuss military tactics and dwelt mostly on the efforts and sacrifices of the Russian people. It became obvious that he was not of a military background, as he focused, primarily on the subjects of political and governmental structure of Russia to the exclusion of the war.

We then invited him to question us about the United States, a country he had visited many times and with which he had some familiarity. His first question was, "What is your country going to do about its Negro problem?" (and this was in April of 1942). I regret to say that none of us came up with an adequate answer other than to suggest it was either an unsolved problem or no problem.

Later, we began to wonder exactly who our Russian friend was—he seemed to know a great deal about the central Soviet government. It emerged that the man, Vladimir Nikolayevich Pavlov, was the interpreter of German, French, and English for Premier Stalin and other senior Soviet officials. One of his duties had been to serve as the interpreter on 13 November 1940, when Hitler met with Foreign Minister Molotov. Pavlov's English was perfect, and our discussion was definitely not limited due to a lack of language capability on the part of our Russian guest.

In early June of 1942 we learned that our mission had been expanded, and we were now a recognized command in a new structure of the U.S. Army. General Marshall ordered the creation of the European Theater of Operations, U.S. Army (nicknamed ETOUSA), tasked with overseeing all American Army operations in Europe, and we were to be part of that command. Its new commander was relatively unknown to the officers in Iceland—his name was Major General Dwight David Eisenhower. ETOUSA headquartered in London, replacing an organization known as U.S. Army Forces, British Isles (USAFBI). For us, it was great news, as we were no longer the lonely vanguard of the U.S. Army in Europe but an integral part of a regular command structure.

The ultimate goal of ETOUSA was to prepare troops for an invasion of the European mainland, which was quickly being overrun by Axis forces. Thus, from that point forward, we of the Iceland Command were no longer looked on as the Army's lone outpost in the Atlantic but, rather, as part of a highly integrated military structure.

Traffic in both personnel and equipment between England and America was in great volume, and because Iceland was a necessary stopover, we had many visitors. One such person, Harry Hopkins, a close confidant of President Roosevelt, was required to spend an extra day in Iceland due to weather conditions, and he presented us with a slight problem. While we were talking in the Officers' Club, he remarked that the "chief" (his reference to the president) had asked Hopkins to bring him one of the famous salmon of Iceland. As it was strictly forbidden to fish or obtain salmon during the off-season, a problem arose. There were no salmon in the shops or anywhere, except the runs now taking place in the rivers. The military and civilian population observed the law to the fullest. We had one friend, however, who might help solve the problem—Kofoed Hansen, who was the chief of police in Reykjavik. We approached him and asked if he could help. Indeed, he had a long list of poachers. It didn't take long for him to pay a visit to one of the offenders, where he "procured" a beautiful large salmon, which we sent on the way to President Roosevelt.

While ETOUSA's role in the eventual attainment of allied victory over Axis forces may be too often unacknowledged, Iceland's introduction to the organization was not inactive. Not only did we have the constant flow of naval convoys crossing the Atlantic, but also we had U.S. aircraft hedgehopping across the Atlantic for duty in England. There were regular flights of bombers and fighters—but it was only one way, and that was to England. On 27 June 1942, the same month that we became a part of ETOUSA, a flight of B-17 bombers ran into foul weather, and one had to make a forced landing on the ice cap of Greenland.

While we knew where the plane was, we could not mount a rescue effort from Iceland, as we had neither aircraft capable of landing on ice nor pilots qualified to attempt such a landing. Fortunately, we were able to call in Colonel Brendt Balchen, the noted pilot who flew Admiral Richard Byrd to the South Pole and had experience in landing on ice caps. He landed on the ice cap in a specially equipped bomber and rescued the stranded crew. Though I had occasion to meet with Balchen a few times, I failed to keep up with him in the drinking arena—in which he was rather excellent!

The American air activity over Iceland was not the only thing increasing in the early summer of 1942. There were also more German Luftwaffe flights, one of which did not return to its base in Norway. U.S. Army Air Force pilots stationed in Iceland shot it down on 14 August 1942, and the event represented the first German plane shot down by a U.S. Army Air Corps plane in World War II.[2]

The German plane, a Focke-Wolf Kurior 200 armed reconnaissance bomber, crash-landed in the mountains of Iceland. I was ordered to lead the expedition to the site of the landing, which took many hours of difficult travel over rugged terrain in bad weather. When we located the site, we found the pilot dead and one crew member wounded. When we searched the plane, great excitement ensued—we had found the codebook currently in use by the German Air Force in the North Atlantic. We believed it was the codebook used to communicate with the German submarines in the area. The codebook had not been damaged in the crash, and I was immediately flown to the U.K. in a B-24 bomber to deliver it personally to the British code breakers at Bletchley Park. This famous code breaking operation worked around the clock to decipher the secret languages of our Axis enemies. Staffers there told me the book contained a code of high interest. We later learned that it proved to be a major asset for the cryptanalysts in the recovery of the system,[3] thereby providing for the quick "breaking" of the German messages. In England, after delivering my treasure to the proper authorities, I was given a room in a small hotel to rest for the night before returning to Iceland. I was bone tired and slept late the next morning, and when I arrived late in the breakfast room, fully expecting to have a full English breakfast, there was only one other person in the room, along with her dog. When I entered, she asked me if I was expecting breakfast, to which I replied, "Yes." She replied, "I am sorry, your breakfast came, and when no one arrived to partake of it, I gave it to my dog." So much for my introduction to the British and their pets—and so much for my breakfast.

The injured German Air Force crew member, recovering back in Iceland, was probably the first German prisoner of war taken by U.S. forces in the European Theater during World War II. He was interrogated and then shipped off to England for internment, but the stir his capture caused among us remained. The American troops in Iceland had scored a first.

Wreckage of the Focke-Wolf Kurior 200, the first German aircraft shot down over Iceland by the U.S. Army Air Force in Europe.

U.S. Army personnel at the wreckage of the German plane shot down over Iceland; Major Hauenstein is second from the right, holding the discovered German codebook.

Wounded German airman who survived the crash of the Focke-Wolfe Kurior 200 aircraft. He was not a very cooperative prisoner.

After that our intelligence personnel in Iceland did not get much time to rest. We soon discovered, by inference, a unique German strategy for protecting ammunition dumps, following an unusual attack. On 31 August 1942, just three weeks after the German bomber had been shot down, I received a frantic phone call from an American intelligence officer stating that the Germans had bombed Akureyri in northern Iceland. When I asked about damage, he said, "There are bodies everywhere!" I asked how many, and the reply was, "Too many to count." After a little more discussion, my contact responded in a jocular vein that the Germans had bombed a cemetery. We were puzzled as to why, and having a suspicion we conducted a reconnaissance survey of the air base in Norway from which the Germans had departed. We learned that they had established ammunition dumps underneath the cemetery adjacent to the air base, apparently believing that Allied forces would not intentionally bomb a graveyard. The assault on the cemetery near the airfield in Akureyri indicated that they believed we had done the same thing, since we did have an airfield in Akureyri. This information was turned over to the British, who reportedly carried out their own bombing of the German air base shortly thereafter.[4]

With America now at war, the Army was desperately in need of experienced officers. One of the first to be called was the G-2 of the Iceland Base Command, Colonel George A. A. Jones, a very capable and experience intelligence officer. Upon his return to America, I became the chief of the G-2 (intelligence) staff unit and took on its intelligence duties.

While I knew that Colonel Jones had been working with Commander Hugh Simpson of the Royal Navy in controlling the German double agents in Iceland, that now became my job. The British controlled these agents for several reasons, which I will get to later, but mainly it was to coordinate the long-range plan for using these agents to pass false information (provided by the British) back to Germany from Iceland regarding a potential invasion of Norway. Obviously we had to assist the British by providing information and ensuring that such information was coordinated by the American Command.

The two German agents were given the code names BEETLE and COBWEB. COBWEB had arrived in Iceland in April of 1942, where he was immediately captured and "turned." BEETLE, the second agent, arrived in Iceland in September of 1943 and was also turned.

COBWEB and BEETLE proved of great value to the long-range planning for Operation OVERLORD (the invasion into the continent of Europe). The OVERLORD plan called for deception in several geographic areas, particularly FORTITUDE NORTH (invasion of Norway), FORTITUDE SOUTH (invasion of the Balkans), and ZEPPLIN SOUTH (invasion of continent at Calais). It was the northern area, FORTITUDE NORTH, a part of the OVERLORD plan, in which we played a part. We were to deceive the Germans into believing that several divisions would be invading Norway. We said that some troops would come from Scotland, and a division would come from Iceland. In reality, at the time of the actual invasion of the continent, we knew that there would be only a small station complement in Iceland. It was our job to deceive the Germans into believing that we had a division (which would be known as the 55th Infantry Division) that would be coming from Iceland and going into Norway for the simultaneous attack of the invasion throughout Europe. In actual fact, the 55th Division existed only on paper.

BEETLE and COBWEB described the buildup of this phantom division in Iceland in their reports home, and they proved invaluable. They were well-known sources fully believed by the Germans and invaluable to the Allied deception plan. They fulfilled their mission, though they were not fully aware of what they were doing. They were not aware of the full extent of the false information provided to them, nor were they aware of the deception plans that were under way.

In a bit of irony, their reports back to Germany were actually transmitted from the quarters of the British commander in Iceland.

I got involved in this unique double-agent program through the director of the Federal Bureau of Investigation (FBI). When J. Edgar Hoover found out about BEETLE and, later, COBWEB, he insisted that they be placed under his control because the FBI was in charge of "turned" German agents in the United States. This demand caused a major debate between the FBI, the U.S. Army, and British intelligence. We in Iceland firmly agreed with the British that it was their program and that the U.S. had nothing to say about how they ran their agents. It was finally—rightly—decided that the U.K. had to control BEETLE and COBWEB, as the U.K. officers were the only ones who would know what intelligence to pass on to the Germans. The deception planning was done by a U.K. group.

I have vivid memories from 1942 and 1943 of the huge armadas that passed by Iceland on their way to resupply the Russians through the port of Murmansk. Hundreds of ships went, and all too often, only a handful of the ships were capable of the return passage. We paid a very high price for those resupply efforts. The convoys had a greater success once the U.K. had the ability to read the German submarine traffic, encrypted on the German cypher device named ENIGMA (a fact that I was not aware of at that time). But for me, the members of the American Merchant Marines who served during World War II will always remain among the war's unsung heroes.

Intelligence operations may have been an important aspect of the Icelandic Base Command following its entry into ETOUSA, but as the months passed, I learned that my tenure as an intelligence officer there was about to end. From the very initiation of hostilities, the Army had been searching through its ranks for experienced men who could be used to fill positions of import in areas of conflict and control across Europe and the Pacific. It was only logical that one of the first places the War Department turned, when looking for officers to staff its new commands, would be the Iceland Base Command, which consisted entirely of regular Army personnel—no draftees.

Early in 1943 General Bonesteel received a message from General Marshall that the Iceland Base Command would be losing some of its seasoned men to other units, units that needed to be fleshed out with practiced regular Army individuals. By this time I had been made G-2 chief of intelligence at the Icelandic Base Command, and I was visited by Colonel Hayes of Washington general headquarters (later to be a general) and told that I would be participating in a top-secret, as-yet-unnamed operation. General Bonesteel did not receive the loss of experienced personnel well. He insisted that such moves would diminish the capability of his base command, and General Marshall, displeased at General Bonesteel's insubordination, initiated action to relieve Bonesteel of his duties. He installed Major General William S. Key, a wealthy oilman from Oklahoma, who commanded the National Guard in that state, as the commander of troops in Iceland. General Marshall was struggling to create a much larger army, but his decision would unwittingly initiate a chain of events that ended in tragedy.

Frank M. Andrews, the American lieutenant general who had temporarily taken over command of ETOUSA in February of 1943, while General Eisenhower was involved in Operation TORCH in North Africa, received a letter from General Marshall directing him to relieve General Bonesteel of his command in Iceland immediately. General Andrews had known General Bonesteel since West Point days—Andrews graduated in 1906 and Bonesteel in 1908—and felt that, in lieu of just forwarding the letter on to General Bonesteel, he would soften the blow and deliver it in person.

On 3 May 1943 General Andrews's plane took off for Iceland with a select party on board: it included among others, Bishop Adna W. Leonard of the Methodist Church; Brigadier General Charles H. Barth, Chief of Staff of ETOUSA; Colonel Morrow Krum, the public affairs officer of ETOUSA, who was a prominent Chicago newspaperman before the war; and Colonel Frank L. Miller, chief of the Plans and Training Division in the Office of the Chief of Chaplains. The plane crashed into a mountain in Iceland, killing all but one of 16 passengers.[5] The only survivor, Staff Sergeant George A. Eisel, the tail gunner, had previously survived a crash in Africa. After this second miraculous escape, he was transferred back to the States.

The official account of the incident states that General Andrews had been conducting aerial reconnaissance surveys of the island, but while examining the flight's wreckage I chanced upon the letter and with it the true reason for his trip. General Andrews was buried in Iceland, and I was in attendance at his funeral.

The bad news about the impending change of command eventually made its way thorough. General Bonesteel, a West Point graduate (also a son and father of West Point graduates) was subsequently relieved by Major General William S. Key,[6] a wealthy oilman from Oklahoma. More different men could not have faced each other on that podium. The gregarious General Key demonstrated just how marked the change of guard would be by remarking off the cuff, "I may not be as good a tactical general as General Bonesteel, but after the war, I'll show him how to make a million dollars, if he comes to Oklahoma." The expression on General Bonesteel's red face was priceless.

General Bonesteel was reassigned as commanding general of Fort Benning, Georgia. Later, in November of 1944, he returned to the European Theater of Operations with the Twelfth Army Group. Subsequently, he was appointed inspector general, European Theater of Operations. While we were once again in the same command, we didn't work together again.

In the meantime, I was learning more about my role in the special mission that had helped incite Bonesteel's ire. I was to accompany the Army on an invasion on the southern coast of the French mainland (Operation ANVIL), to take place simultaneously with a larger landing in the northern region of that country. I was to serve as a conduit, keeping the troops in the southern area of France informed as to the progress of American forces simultaneously landing in the northern region of that country. I was extremely apprehensive as this foray would mark my first real move into combat. Had my intelligence work left me adequately prepared?

Upon my arrival in London, where I was to be briefed further, I learned these landings were part of a fictional operation meant to divert German attention away from the Russian front. This news came to my great relief!

I soon learned that the ETOUSA command still had a few ideas up its metaphorical sleeve for me. In August of 1943, I was assigned to work in the intelligence division of ETOUSA, located at 20 Grosvenor Square. This assignment was more to my liking, and I was eager to put this knowledge to use for a wider audience, which encompassed the entire ETOUSA command.

Thus ended my time in the North Atlantic, but not the mission of the troops stationed there. Americans in Iceland were to have a unique role in solidifying the strategy of Allied forces during the D-day invasion. Our forces in Iceland helped convince the Germans that our fictitious troops (the 55th Infantry Division), along with the troops in the northern area of Scotland, were ostensibly poised to invade Norway, timed to occur simultaneously with the actual assault on the French coast. Our two double agents, COBWEB and BEETLE, had a key role in the deception. They took care to ensure that the Germans knew what the mission of our phantom division was to be and approximately when it was to take place. It was apparent from decryptions of German army coded messages that the ruse worked!

Throughout the remainder of the war I remained aware of the Iceland operation and to this day remain very proud to have been a part of it.

Official Army photograph of the recovery effort after the crash of General Andrews's plane, 3 May 1943. Only one person survived.

Official Army photograph of the funeral for General Andrews held in Iceland. Major Hauenstein is the fourth officer from the right.

NOTES

1. In January of 1942, the U.S. Marines received orders to begin returning to the United States. The final Marine contingent sailed from Reykjavik on 9 March 1942. Thus ended the presence of major Marine elements in the European Theater.

2. U.S. air operations in Europe were initiated on 4 July 1942. It was not until 17 August that the U.S. Air Force conducted its first air attack against Europe. Lt. Elza S. Shahan and Lt. Joseph D. Shaffer, the pilots who shot down the bomber over Iceland, were both awarded the Silver Star for their actions.

3. The codebook used by the German Air Force contained about 1,000 items. It was encoded by using a three-digit number for a phrase, word, or character, then re-enciphered using a substitution table. A retired member of the Bletchley Park staff, Miss Lavall (now Mrs. Cunningham), was the person who initially received such codebooks at Bletchley. She recalls great excitement whenever they were received and also remembers receiving more than one that was bloodstained.

4. The official Icelandic version is that it was not a bombing at all, merely German bombers who were lightening their loads prior to returning to their base in Norway. The bombs were intended to land in the sea but instead landed in Iceland. Iceland has no record of a cemetery being involved. Another possible story is that the bombing was in some way retribution for the shooting down of the German bomber on 17 August (just two weeks before the bombing). Could it not be that the German crew decided to lighten its load in retribution? We will never know, but the sequence surely suggests that.

5. Those killed in the crash, in addition to General Andrews and Bishop Leonard, were Brigadier General Charles H. Barth, chief of staff to General Andrews; Colonel Murrow Krum, public affairs officer, European headquarters; Chaplain Colonel Frank L. Miller, chief of chaplains; Lt. Colonel Fred A. Chapman; Major Theodore C. Torman; Major Robert H. Humphrey; Captain James E. Gott; Master Sergeant Lloyd C. Weir; Technical Sergeant Kenneth A. Jeffers; and Staff Sergeant Paul. H. McQueen. The only survivor was Staff Sergeant George A. Eisel.

6. William S. Key had served with the U.S. Army in World War I and in 1940 was a major general in command of the 45th Division of the National Guard. In October of 1942 he became the provost marshal general for the ETOUSA in London and served in that capacity until he was transferred to the Iceland Command. He later headed the U.S. Military Control Commission for Hungary from December of 1944 until July of 1946.

European Theater of Operations, U.S. Army (ETOUSA)

Organizational Concepts

When I arrived in London I was assigned to the European Theater of Operations, United States Army, known by the acronym of ETOUSA. I knew of the organization, because once the U.S. entered the war, the U.S. Army Command in Iceland became part of ETOUSA. I was also aware that General Marshall as chief of staff of the Army had dictated that for the period of the war in Europe there would be one command element over all the U.S. Army forces deployed to Europe, and that organization would be ETOUSA. I was a little in awe of my assignment to such an organization.

I have observed over the years that for many of the historians and military minds who study World War II, ETOUSA is merely an acronym for an organization that served very little purpose for the war effort in Europe. So before I relate any of my specific experiences while serving with ETOUSA, I think it is important to understand exactly what constituted ETOUSA, how it functioned, and how it interfaced with the Supreme Headquarters, Allied Expeditionary Force (SHAEF) Command.

Organizations established by the military to answer specific wartime needs often disappear once the need has ended. Others are frequently overshadowed by a higher echelon and are later lost to history. The American military organization known as ETOUSA, active throughout the entire World War II period in Europe, is such an organization. It was the top U.S. Army command structure in Europe from 1942 to 1945, but today in the modern histories of World War II it is barely mentioned. For veterans of ETOUSA, like myself, the apparent lack of understanding and appreciation for the mission of ETOUSA has been a continual source of frustration and disbelief. With that in mind, before the specifics of my assignment with ETOUSA are highlighted, it is important to understand the environment in which I lived—that of ETOUSA.

I hope that the following sections on the organizational concepts and the functions of ETOUSA, specifically the G-2 operations, will provide adequate background and appreciation for the specific events that follow.

For the American forces in the war in Europe, there were two distinct command structures, which led to considerable confusion and ambiguity. First there was the European Theater of Operations, United States Army (ETOUSA) which, in mid-1942 was the acronym given to all the operations of the U.S. Army in the European Theater. The commanding general of ETOUSA was the United States senior commander of all U.S. Army forces in Europe, eventually amounting to three Army Groups, seven Armies, the 8th and 15th Air Armies, and the Services of Supply (SOS). It was to this command staff that I was assigned on my arrival in England. The activities of ETOUSA were in support of the U.S. troops only from Army Group level down. In essence, ETOUSA was the "Pentagon" for the U.S. Army forces in Europe. Once the U.S. Armies were deployed they had their own command structures, and ETOUSA only became involved in activities that encompassed all of the Armies or in cases of disputes between two U.S. Armies. The British Army had no similar command structure for their forces in the European Theater. Their forces were not geographically separated from the central U.K. command structure and therefore required no intermediate structure. For example, it was quite common for General Bernard L. Montgomery to fly over to the U.K. when and if the situation required his presence, a luxury our U.S. commanding general did not have. And by the time of the invasion of Europe, the blitz of London had eased, making such trips not too risky.

Later, in January of 1944, as the Allied combined command took form, a new multinational command came into being—that of Supreme Headquarters Allied Expeditionary Force (SHAEF)—of which ETOUSA was the U.S. element. The new organization absorbed COSSAC (Chief of Staff to Supreme Allied Command), which had served for the planning of OVERLORD. SHAEF was responsible for the activities of all the Allied forces to include American, British, French, Canadian, and all other "free" forces involved in defeating the Nazis in Europe. The person named to be the supreme commander of the Allied Expeditionary Force, General Dwight D. Eisenhower, at the same time reassumed command of ETOUSA. He served two masters— the Allies through the SHAEF Command and the American forces through ETOUSA. For the remainder of the war he continued to cross boundaries between the two organizations, often treating them as one organization. It was not infrequent that ETOUSA staff elements such as the G-2 (where I was assigned) were tasked with a project by the SHAEF chief of staff. This boundary crossing was perhaps a necessity, but it caused a great deal of confusion for the American forces.

To really understand the American or ETOUSA functions during the European phase of World War II, it is beneficial to begin almost at the inception of the American entry into the war. When the United States entered the war, the American presence in Europe basically consisted of Major General James E. Chaney, with a small staff, assigned to the U.K. as a military observer. His function was to liaise with the British, in order to present the early U.S. views on the war effort and to report to the U.S. what was happening in the British military. The official title for his organization was United States Army Forces, British Isles, or USAFBI.

By early spring of 1942, the Plans Division of the U.S. Army, under the supervision of General Eisenhower, had developed a master plan for the defeat of Germany in Europe. The plan calling for the invasion of Europe, codenamed ROUND UP, in the spring of 1943, required British support and commitment before it could be put into motion. By this time, General Marshall had become disenchanted with the performance of General James E. Chaney in London—he did not appear to be taking his job seriously enough for General Marshall—and decided he was not the man to present the ROUND UP plan to the British. Eisenhower, in contrast, had been a major force in developing the overall strategy, and in Marshall's mind Eisenhower was the man to do the job.

In May of 1942 General Eisenhower flew to London with a twofold mission: first, to gauge the U.K. commitment to the U.S. plan (ROUND UP) for the invasion of Europe; second, to report back to General Marshall on the performance of General Chaney. It was during this visit that General Eisenhower met Winston Churchill for the first time, and an almost instant friendship developed. General Eisenhower returned from his trip very disenchanted, both with the U.K.'s reaction to the War Department plan and with the performance of General Chaney, who he recommended be replaced. In the meantime, Churchill had wired General Marshall that the British High Command had been very impressed with General Eisenhower and his dedication to the Allied alliance.

Within a month of his return from London (8 June 1942) Eisenhower briefed General Marshall on a draft directive for the U.S. Army commander of the European Theater of Operations (ETO), a name Ike had given the London Command (quickly to be nicknamed ETOUSA). In the initial draft the commander was listed as General James Chaney. This new command was recommended to replace USAFBI, which had been established by General Order No. 1, Hq., USAFBI, dated 8 January 1942.

General Marshall approved the draft directive with one major change: the commander would not be Major General Chaney but would be Major General Eisenhower (General Order No. 6, Hq., ETOUSA, 24 June 1942). General Marshall was fully aware that the war in Europe would be an Allied effort, but he was adamant that the U.S. forces would maintain an independent U.S. Army headquarters in Europe. When ETOUSA was activated, the Iceland Base Command became part of the new organization and no longer a separate command.

The initial mission of the new ETOUSA organization was to prepare the American Army for its role in the invasion of the European continent, as agreed between the British and American governments. This invasion was to be the main strategic effort in the ultimate defeat of Nazi Germany.

The role of the commander of ETO was defined in OPD (Operations Planning Division) Directive 27 dated 19 June 1942, with the subject, Commanding General USAFBI Designated as Commanding General, European Theater, AGO (Adjutant General's Office) Established the Command, as excerpted below:

> The Commanding General, European Theater . . . will command all U.S. Army Forces and personnel now in, or hereafter dispatched, to the European Theater of Operations, including any part of the Marine Corps therein which may be detached for service with the Army.
>
> By agreement between the Navy and War Departments, planning and operational control will be exercised by the Commanding General over all U.S. Navy Forces assigned to this Theater.
>
> Subject to such limitations within the British Isles as are necessary to avoid any violations of British sovereignty,

the Commanding General, European Theater, is charged with the tactical, territorial and administrative duties of a theater commander.
    The mission of the Commanding General, European Theater, will be to prepare for and carry on military operations in the European Theater against the Axis Powers and their Allies.

While General Eisenhower initially served solely as the commander of the American organization ETOUSA, in July of 1942 he quickly organized an Allied forces headquarters, which was a consolidated U.S./U.K. headquarters with himself as commander. His dual role as commander of ETOUSA and the joint U.S./U.K. headquarters led to considerable confusion and organizational conflict. We would frequently ask ourselves the question, "Are we being tasked for ETOUSA or for U.S./U.K. purposes?"
    When Eisenhower was named the supreme commander for the invasion of North Africa,[1] he replaced himself as the commanding general of ETOUSA and appointed Lt. General Frank Andrews to the position (4 February 1943).
    As the role of the U.S. Army in Europe continued to expand, it was decided that a new command should be formed to encompass the geographic area of North Africa, which was an early target for Allied invasion. That command, formed on 4 February 1943, was called NATOUSA (the North African Theater of Operations, U.S. Army), with Brigadier General T. B. Larkin named as the first commander. Almost immediately the geographic boundaries of ETOUSA were changed to exclude Spain, Italy, and several of the Mediterranean islands, and these areas were incorporated into the NATOUSA area of operations. As with ETOUSA, these commands were responsible only for the support of U.S. Army units in their geographic areas.
    General Andrews served as commanding general of ETOUSA until his untimely death in a plane crash in Iceland, as discussed in earlier pages. Lt. General Jacob L. Devers was named as his replacement (3 May 1943), and he served in that capacity until 8 January 1944 when General Eisenhower once again assumed command of ETOUSA.[2] General Devers then became the chief of NATOUSA under U.K. General Sir Henry Maitland Wilson, the commander of the

Mediterranean Theater of Operations (MTO). On 16 January 1944 General Eisenhower was named supreme commander of the Allied Expeditionary Force, Europe. He also continued to command ETOUSA for the remainder of the war period. General W. Beddell Smith became the chief of staff for both SHAEF and ETOUSA, serving initially as the nominal head of ETOUSA under General Eisenhower's direction. On 25 January 1944 Lt. General Ben Lear was assigned to ETOUSA as the deputy theater commander to General Eisenhower. One of General Lear's primary responsibilities was to train infantrymen and to move large numbers of soldiers into combat. The command structure of ETOUSA is shown in the following chart.

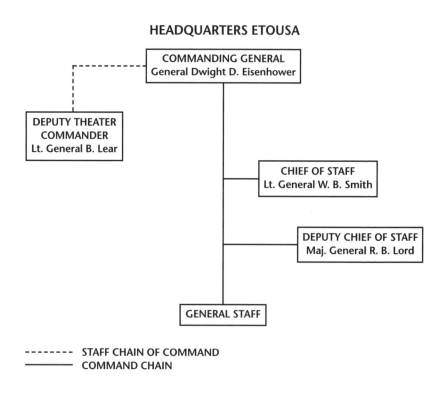

HEADQUARTERS ETOUSA

- COMMANDING GENERAL
  General Dwight D. Eisenhower
- DEPUTY THEATER COMMANDER
  Lt. General B. Lear
- CHIEF OF STAFF
  Lt. General W. B. Smith
- DEPUTY CHIEF OF STAFF
  Maj. General R. B. Lord
- GENERAL STAFF

- - - - - - - STAFF CHAIN OF COMMAND
——————— COMMAND CHAIN

ETOUSA became the U.S. Army command solely for activities in Europe. The U.S. Army activities in the Mediterranean area (to include Spain and Italy) were a separate command—the MTO—under SHAEF, with NATOUSA as the U.S. Army element in that command. General Devers was replaced as commanding general of NATOUSA by General Joseph T. McNarney on 23 October 1944, and on 1 November 1944 NATOUSA was redesignated as MTOUSA (Mediterranean Theater of Operations, U.S. Army).

Organizational problems continued to plague both groups, in part because General Eisenhower tended to use personnel from both the U.S. and Allied Commands interchangeably, as required. His problem was a shortage of qualified personnel, so he tapped all sources as necessary. Although this was an expedient option for him, the staffs frequently were confused as to who tasked them, and the troops were confused—to whom did they report?

For General Eisenhower, the culmination came on 16 January 1944, when he assumed the position of supreme commander of SHAEF. Now the time had come to dissolve the joint U.S./U.K. headquarters, known as the Allied Forces headquarters, and establish a headquarters, Supreme Allied Expeditionary Force, which absorbed the COSSAC (Chief of Staff, Supreme Allied Command) organization. Ike decided to move the new SHAEF headquarters out of London to Bushy Park near Kingston, which geographically separated him from ETOUSA.

COSSAC had been formed in March of 1943 as a joint U.S./U.K. group charged with planning for the invasion of the continent by the Allied forces. U.K. Lt. General F. E. Morgan was the head of this group. Although COSSAC was later absorbed into SHAEF, General Morgan continued as the chief of staff throughout the war period. COSSAC had a small contingent and worked with G-3 ETOUSA, to which I was initially assigned, and also later G-2 ETOUSA.

At the height of the European campaign, SHAEF's total strength was 16,312. Nearly 1,600 of those serving at SHAEF were U.S. officers; another 1,229 were U.K. officers; and the remainder were U.S./U.K. enlisted personnel. There were also military missions assigned to SHAEF from France, the Netherlands, Belgium, Denmark, Norway, and eventually the Soviet Union.

For the U.S. forces the structure was now General Eisenhower as the supreme allied commander (SHAEF) with authority over all Allied forces, as well as commanding general of ETOUSA. General W. B.

Smith served as his chief of staff for ETOUSA, with jurisdiction over the U.S. Army force in Europe. In reality, General Eisenhower continued his practice of using personnel from both organizations on an as-required basis.

By January of 1944 it was evident that the supply and communications functions were becoming a critical element in planning for the invasion of Europe. In response, General Eisenhower consolidated headquarters of ETOUSA with headquarters of Services of Supply (SOS) (known in the European Theater as COM Z) into what can best be called a joint command, ETOUSA/COM Z. There was theoretically now one organization responsible for all phases of the war effort for the American troops. ETOUSA had the overall staff functions, and COM Z had the responsibility for the supply and servicing of the troops. My staff in ETOUSA G-2 (intelligence) became very familiar with all the local geography for passable bridges and roadways for delivering supplies.

The new organization had developmental problems, particularly as regards the staff functions. Finally on 27 June 1944 it was established that the ETOUSA staffs involved in the merger of SOS and ETOUSA were G-1 (administration) and G-4 (supply). We of the G-2 (intelligence) and the G-3 (operations) staffs, as well as other organizations such as Signals Corps and Ordinance that did not pertain to COM Z, remained strictly under ETOUSA. Certainly this was not a very neat and tidy organizational concept.

Based on the above concept, the problem arose that the two organizations were never completely merged. General Eisenhower named Major General John C. H. Lee, the SOS commander, to be the deputy theater commander of ETOUSA to include COM Z, but each of the two parts (ETOUSA and COM Z) retained their own organizational structure. As an ETOUSA staff member, I was well aware that U.S. field commanders looked on this new structure with a great deal of dislike. They knew that General Eisenhower was totally involved with his duties as supreme commander, SHAEF, and therefore by default his deputy commander for ETOUSA would be the de facto commander of U.S. forces in Europe. Commanders continued to react adversely to reporting to Ike through a "supply officer" and not a tactical field officer. They frequently went around General Lee through General Smith, chief of staff, which only complicated matters. General Eisenhower solved this problem by adding the phrase "for supply only" to General Lee's title as deputy commander. The outcome was that

General Lee handled the supply functions and General Smith continued to be responsible for the overall functions of ETOUSA in general staff support of the U.S. Army in Europe.

The two organizations under General Eisenhower's control, while operationally necessary—one for all the Allies and one for the U.S. alone—gave rise to constant confusion. As an example, the General Board, ETO Report No. 2, titled *Study of the Organization of European Theater of Operations*, contains the following paragraph:

> 52. *Relationship between SHAEF and ETOUSA.* The Supreme Commander also commanded ETOUSA and the major commands of ETOUSA were placed under the operational direction of the Supreme Commander. This resulted in the 12th Army Group and the 6th Army Group being dealt with directly without the necessity of utilizing ETOUSA command channels. Similarly when necessary, SHAEF dealt directly with the Communications Zone. Although matters of purely American interest were handled between the War Department and headquarters, ETOUSA, those with direct operational implications were closely coordinated with the Supreme Headquarters. However, the dividing line as to functions between the two headquarters and responsibilities were often determined by personal agreements between the two agencies when the necessity arose, or by the direction of the Chief of Staff. This resulted in the sections of the headquarters of SHAEF assuming dual functions and interests within the affairs of ETOUSA when their primary interest and responsibility clearly rested in matters pertaining to Allied affairs.

The preceding paragraph clearly states that the "Supreme Commander also commanded ETOUSA and the major commands of ETOUSA." ETOUSA remained virtually a separate organization not directly in the chain of command of COM Z. I was in charge of the intelligence section of the ETOUSA G-2 section and never served under or for COM Z, although I did provide intelligence support.

The German surrender in May of 1945 meant that the mission of the Allied Command had been completed, and therefore on 14 July the SHAEF Command was officially terminated. The mission of ETOUSA, however, continued beyond the surrender, as on 17 June

1945 Hq. ETOUSA was tasked by General Order No. 128 to conduct a complete analysis of the Allied war effort.

Finally, on 1 July 1945 Hq. ETOUSA was redesignated Hq. USFET (U.S. Forces European Theater), with a main headquarters in the I. G. Farben building in Frankfurt, Germany, where I served for a short period of time. There was also a rear headquarters in Paris, France (General Order No. 130, Hq. ETOUSA, 30 June 1945). General Eisenhower was named the commanding general of U.S. forces in the European Theater, commander-in-chief of U.S. forces of occupation in Germany, and representative of the United States on the Allied Control Council of Germany.[3]

Between ETOUSA's establishment in 1942 and its redesignation as USFET in 1945, ETOUSA had been a critical element for the U.S. Army in Europe. It had provided staff support for the planning of the Allied invasion of Western Europe; performed administrative and service functions for U.S. Army troops; provided equipment and facilities in the U.K., Iceland, North Africa, and Western Europe—all those always in the shadow of SHAEF.

With the end of the war and the new mission for USFET, many of the officers and men of ETOUSA were officially transferred to headquarters, COM Z, an integral part of U.S. forces, European Theater, headquartered in Frankfurt, Germany.

General Order No. 38, USFET, 20 March 1947, redesignated Hq. USFET as headquarters, European Command (HQ EUCOM), effective 15 March 1947. ETOUSA had now become the occupier of its previous enemy.

NOTES

1. The War Department notified Eisenhower of this change in cables dated 2, 6, and 7 February 1943. Eisenhower activated the North African Theater and assumed command by General Orders No. 1, dated 4 February 1943.

2. Reassignment was done by War Department cable dated 31 December 1943. Eisenhower reassumed command of ETOUSA on 16 January 1944 by General Order No. 4, same date.

3. Reorganization of U.S. Army in Europe accomplished by War Department cable dated 29 June 1945.

Duty in Europe, Pre-OVERLORD

August 1943 to June 1944

I arrived in Europe in August of 1943 knowing only that I would be assigned to the staff of ETOUSA (European Theater of Operations, U.S. Army) in London. At that time, General Devers was ETOUSA commanding general, while General Eisenhower was involved in the Mediterranean campaign. Duty in London was very different from duty in Iceland. It was a return to the civilized world—but what a different civilized world it was! While I had become accustomed to British military, their language and methods, I was not prepared for British civilians. They were a little different: they drove on the wrong side of the road, "knocked you up" in the morning, and spoke a language quite different from what we Americans called "English." And on the military front, I soon discovered that I was now part of the actual organization that was planning the major initiatives for the remainder of the European war effort. It was both exhilarating and daunting—would I be up to the task? I was determined to meet the challenge.

Assignments came rapidly, and within a short time, I had achieved the rank of colonel at the age of 32. It was an achievement I was proud of, but one that presented some drawbacks. I had a youthful face, which meant that I had to work hard to get people to listen to me—and that I'd better have my facts straight when I did.

Upon arrival, I was initially assigned to the G-3 (operations) group, to be involved in the intelligence aspects for both Operations ANVIL and OVERLORD. However, ANVIL was delayed, and after only a two-month period, canceled. I was then reassigned to the G-2 (intelligence) staff under Brigadier General Bryan Conrad, ETOUSA, G-2, to carry on the intelligence responsibilities in support of our Army units. I was both pleased and a little intimidated by the assignment. The implications were horrendous. The TRIDENT Conference in Washington, D.C., held on 12 May 1943, had decided on 1 May 1944 as the D-day for OVERLORD, the invasion of Europe. Therefore, I knew that, at least for the next year, we would be very busy. Our military efforts in North Africa had been accomplished with the German surrender there on 13 May 1943, thus allowing us to focus all our efforts on OVERLORD.

My branch of ETOUSA was composed of 17 officers, 1 warrant officer, and 19 enlisted personnel, with numerous personnel in related subsections also under my command. We maintained control of all intelligence matters related to the American Army Command level in Europe. We served as a reservoir of data requiring the turning of information into intelligence, and we responded to a wide range of actions that required our intelligence input. Our responsibilities demanded that intelligence be both classified as to its security—restricted, confidential, secret, or top secret—and its distribution to the appropriate commands was carefully monitored. We were covering new territory, as America was planning the engagement of numerous divisions, corps, army, and army groups, and the intelligence "need-to-know" was vital to the various commands. What might be essential information at the command levels was necessarily distinct from the intelligence requirements of Services of Supply (SOS) and other special units. Rarely, however, did we distribute beneath Army echelons.

The sources of information and intelligence passing through my branch were numerous. Information came from a diverse array, including international affairs, reports from technical experts, agent activities, combat activities in all theaters of operation, and enemy orders of battle. We supplied much of the data for the major war rooms and their mapping.

Staffers focused on various types of intelligence activities, including engineer intelligence, which required us to plot maps and to conduct detailed studies of rivers and other geographical markers; technical intelligence, which required us to ferret out information about scientific advances in chemical warfare, rocket development, and nuclear research; prisoner-of-war (POW) interrogations; and coordination with counterintelligence and subversive intelligence. My principle duties at ETOUSA were to supervise each of these areas and to find openings in our department for the many officers who had just finished general staff school in the States and were coming to Europe as majors and lieutenant colonels. My branch also handled photo interpretation and interrogation of POWs, and notified SHAEF whenever it received information of interest to the combined Allied forces, not just to American Army troops stationed overseas. There were few manuals, texts, or even higher-level courses I could look to, to learn about such matters—a vestige of the mistrust of intelligence fostered by Secretary of War Henry L. Stimson more than a decade earlier—so all this work was done largely through rapid on-the-job training and using existing experience.

Brigadier General Bryan Conrad, the ETOUSA G-2, and I were the only ETOUSA intelligence officers accredited to have all echelons of classified material—ultra, most secret, top secret, confidential, restricted, and so on. I chose to stay away from Bletchley Park, where the ENIGMA traffic was broken by British cryptographers, but I received their reports and was aware of the importance of their operation. I was also aware of the small group of Americans assisting the British there.[1] My contact with this group was through Colonel Telford Taylor, their commander, who later went on to become the chief U.S. prosecutor of the war crimes trials at Nuremburg.

In addition to U.S. staffing, I had a French general staff colonel assigned to me as a liaison officer, as well as a U.K. member of the British Army, Lord (Major) Jacob Rothschild. We also worked with one highly talented technical expert, Dr. H. P. Robertson, the U.S. scientific adviser to General Eisenhower, and a member of my group.

The role of my branch was not the day-to-day tactical intelligence gathering. That was for the tactical units. We were responsible for the gathering, processing, and dissemination of intelligence that affected the entire command. For example, once the Army units were in Europe, my branch had to ensure that the intelligence apparatus we had established for the units was functioning and that we responded to their intelligence requirements; at the same time, we were involved in special projects at the request of General Eisenhower pertinent to the U.S. commands.

The British, through COSSAC, had been working for several months on the planned invasion into Europe. The plan was given the name of OVERLORD, and its draft was sent down to our headquarters, where it was to be reviewed in greater detail by the G-3 section, as well as the G-2, under the leadership of Colonel William Harris and his assistant Major Ralph Ingersol. General Devers was commanding ETOUSA at the time, and he coordinated the review and discovered some discrepancies that made it unacceptable to him: mainly that the plan would be impossible to carry out because we lacked the necessary landing craft. It was a difficult situation because all of the landing craft being produced in America at that time were ordered by Admiral Ernest J. King to be sent to the theater of operations in the Pacific where the war was an island-hopping scenario. The British, by contrast, had given their manufacturing facilities over to the production of aircraft, an essential element for the protection of Britain. Major Ingersol, a long-time friend of Harry Hopkins, volunteered to go to Washington and see what he could do to get additional production or a redistribution of the landing crafts, in order to carry out the plan of OVERLORD. Having been the editor of a New York newspaper, Ingersol also had known Roosevelt. However, it was Harry Hopkins, President Roosevelt's staff assistant, whom he visited about this critical situation. Upon his return to Europe, Ingersol advised that Hopkins had apparently convinced the president to divert some of the manufactured landing craft to the European theater, despite the objections of Admiral King, who continued to press the need for landing craft in the Pacific Theater. Production of the necessary landing craft to carry out the OVERLORD was scheduled and accomplished.

In December of 1943, at the Cairo Conference, President Roosevelt announced his decision regarding which American general would be the commander of the Allied forces to invade Germany. That man was to be General Dwight D. Eisenhower. His deputy would be British Air Marshall Sir Arthur W. Tedder, and his British Ground Commander would be General Bernard Montgomery. His G-2 would be U.K. General Morgan (who had been the head of COSSAC) and his chief of staff would be General W. Bedell Smith. General Eisenhower shortly returned to London to begin preparations for the invasion of Europe.

Not long after Eisenhower's return, I was approached by a senior American officer and was completely taken aback by his request. He was looking for an American aide-de-camp to serve with General Montgomery. Since I had held that position with General Bonesteel in Iceland, would I be interested in being considered for the same post with General Montgomery? I wasn't quite sure he was serious, but I quickly and firmly declined the honor.

It did not take long for me to realize that General Eisenhower was absolutely the right man to head the Allied Command. No one else was as good at fostering cooperation between elements unaccustomed to working together. He also, due to his early athletic training, had a strong physical stamina, which provided him the ability to work long hours without hindering his decision-making capabilities. He displayed great leadership.

Soon after I arrived, I began to hear stories about General Eisenhower and his driver Kay Summersby. I had seen her around headquarters and knew that she was a very attractive woman, who served as his aide and driver. I believe that the female U.K. drivers had a dual mission. Yes, they drove for senior American officials—even I had a driver (but being of a lower rank, my driver was not terribly attractive!). It struck me, however, that these women were generally very attractive, well spoken, upper-middle class, and intelligent. Could they have been assigned by U.K. intelligence to keep the British informed as to what the Americans were up to? I think so. One specific case comes to mind. The American G-2 who was in England when I arrived, a brigadier general, made a tactical mistake. He went on an inspection trip with his driver, and during the trip, proceeded to have a romantic tryst with her. When they returned, she reported him to his superior, and not for the romantic activity, but for the fact that he left highly classified material adrift during the interlude. He was immediately demoted and returned to the United States.

One of my early assignments provided me with an opportunity to play a minor part in the development of the Allied plans for the invasion of Europe. I was selected as one of the American representatives to attend a planning session at the Lord Mountbatten School at Largs in northern Scotland. I had never heard of the school or of Largs, Scotland, but after a little research, I discovered that, when Mountbatten was named as the chief of combined operations in October of 1941, he had established this school to be known as the Combined Operations School. The area was selected for its terrain, which was very similar to that of the European coastal area where the teams might be attempting raids.

The conference was a followup to a June 1943 session (code-named RATTLE), chaired by Mountbatten, where the senior commanders had developed the basic plans for the invasion of Europe. It was this meeting that decided where the initial assault would take place and approximately the date of the action as required by the U.S. and U.K. governments. One of the prime factors in the selection process for the landing area was that it should contain sufficient port facilities to maintain a force of some 30 to 40 divisions.

Attendees were field officers from the Army, Air, and the Navy, as well as military representatives from England, South Africa, Australia, Canada, New Zealand, and the United States. The discussions were wide-ranging and fruitful. Working from plans possibly to be used for an invasion of the continent, the instructors sought the opinions of the officers from the branches of service likely to execute the plan. For example, the initial plans we saw called for a certain number of flights to be made by pilots during the course of the invasion, and those plans immediately drew a rebuke from the British air commodore, who cited that, during the Battle of Britain he made more than twice that number of flights and was still good for the next days' flying. The clear implication was that we could use a greater number of flights for air support during the invasion than had been proposed in the initial plans of the instructors. The same sort of discussions occurred about the possibility of using battleships in the channel. I remember being quite adamant myself regarding the use of battleships because we certainly needed the 16-inch guns to target the fortified cliffs in France. This question drew a heated discussion from many, particularly from some instructors, who said that it was too dangerous to have a battleship in the channel. They felt it would be far too vulnerable to artillery and would jeopardize the battleship. However, my team during the course of this conference prevailed with the requirement that battleships be used in the invasion to give the necessary artillery support.

As a grand finale to the seminar, British commandoes staged a mock exercise in the fjords and cliffs near Largs. They used live ammunition, and the effect on the audience, at least for me, was very dramatic. It really drove home the magnitude of the task ahead.

Over the next few months the planning continued. Among my new assignments was one that led me to Oxford, where I worked with a group of academics involved in a special study for the Allies. I had always been proud of my Army career, but working with world-class professors gave me a particular high.

Back in London, I was faced with the problem of turning newly arrived officers into professional military intelligence operatives. Training was a challenge and can be understood with a little background.

All through the late 1930s, Army regulations had failed to allocate any specific intelligence training functions to the Military Intelligence Department (MID), and the War Department Training Directive for

1939 still carried no mention of combat intelligence training. The only training, so to speak, was the standard practice of having one or more representatives of MID attend the larger Army maneuvers as official observers. These observers carefully noted the role and functions of the intelligence personnel. Finally, in late 1941, the question of Army training for military intelligence had reached such a point that an Army-wide conference was scheduled. It was scheduled to begin in Washington, D.C., on 8 December 1941. It obviously did not happen.

General Omar Bradley comments on the U.S. Army's training of military intelligence officers in his biography, *A Soldier's Story*, gave further credence to the lack of preparedness of the U.S. Army in the area of intelligence. He states:

> In their intelligence activities at AFHq., the British easily out-stripped their American colleagues. The tedious years of prewar study the British had devoted to areas throughout the world gave them a vast advantage, which we never overcame. *The American army's long neglect of intelligence training was soon reflected by the ineptness of our initial undertakings. For too many years in the preparation of officers for command assignments, we had overlooked the need for specialization in such activities as intelligence.* It is unrealistic to assume that every officer has the capacity and the inclination for field command. Many are uniquely qualified for staff–intelligence duties and indeed would prefer to devote their careers to those tasks. Yet instead of grooming qualified officers for intelligence assignments, we rotated them through conventional duty tours, making correspondingly little use of their special talents. Misfits frequently found themselves assigned to intelligence duties. And in some stations G-2 became a dumping ground for officers ill suited to line command. I recall how scrupulously I avoided the branding that came with an intelligence assignment in my own career. *Had it not been for the uniquely qualified reservists who so capably filled so many of our intelligence jobs throughout the war, the army would have found itself badly pressed for competent intelligence personnel.* (italics added.)

Therein lay my problem. It fell to us, with some exceptions, to train those troops designated to be tactical military intelligence officers in support of American Army units as they went into action in Europe. Manuals, texts, and courses in how to conduct military intelligence were all in the developmental stages, so innovation and creativity counted a great deal. We learned from our mistakes, as well as our successes.

The cadre of officers destined to be assigned to tactical military intelligence duties that arrived in England had some interesting characteristics. I noted that many who came to me were Ivy League, and among their ranks many were lawyers. One man I specifically remember was William Jackson, who later became associated with the Central Intelligence Agency (on my recommendation). Jackson was typical of several highly qualified individuals who were given Army commissions without military training. His first assignment was to the highly classified ULTRA operation, working basically under the control of the British at Bletchley Park while being detailed to certain American Army units. I recall Jackson, upon his arrival in London and within a few days of reporting in, asking me how the intelligence units functioned. Later he served with distinction with the 12th Army Group.

The influx of field grade officers awaiting assignment to yet-to-be-formed and newly arrived Corps, Army, and Army Groups presented a logistical problem. While the new arrivals awaited their specific assignments, we gave them a few days leave to see London, and upon return, we held briefing sessions.

On one occasion, I had my staff prepare a paper incorporating all the knowledge we had accumulated on the Germans that reflected their knowledge of our forces and the potential when and where of the Allied invasion on the continent. We had accumulated much data in this regard through German broadcasts, signal intercepts, agent reports, and photo reconnaissance, among other sources. We gave this information to our new officers, who at this point had not been briefed on the invasion plan, and asked them to predict where and when the Germans believed the invasion would come.

After a two-day exercise we had the officers present their individual views in a written report, and the results turned in. To my utter amazement, several had detailed metrological and tidal factors, areas of coastal landings, and numerous other plans that accompanied the possible invasion. Their predictions were so close to the actual OVER-LORD plan, that I let no one see the papers. Then I merely thanked the temporary students, sent them to the War Room for new briefings, and shredded their reports. D-day was too close.

The remaining days of 1943 and the first half of 1944 were spent gathering intelligence in preparation for the D-day invasion. Agents used all manner of resources in an effort to ferret out clues to Axis location and strength and to transmit fallacious information to the enemy about our own location and strength. Of particular importance was technical intelligence. If the Germans were allowed to outpace American technological development in firearms, vehicles, and other weapons of destruction, all of our invasion efforts would be undermined. Likewise, we needed to ensure that our own troops maintained adequate know-how to eliminate Axis facilities they would encounter as they made their way across Europe.

The types of technical intelligence we engaged in were numerous. Reports from French and Polish underground organizations proved invaluable in learning about the research that Axis scientists were conducting in Peenemuende, in northern Germany. We had isolated the region as the area where they were developing V1 and V2 rockets to be used in attacks on England and other regions in Europe. The V1s, or "buzz bombs," were, for all practical purposes, planes packed with explosives that operated sans pilots. V2s were tanks of highly flammable liquid oxygen. Aerial reconnaissance would reveal the location of temporary V1 and V2 launching pads and would prove invaluable in helping us carry out bombing raids on that area in August of 1943.[2] It would also reveal the permanent launch sites in the Watten area of France. We asked an engineer at what stage of the construction would the structure be most vulnerable to an air attack. His answer was to wait until the concrete was freshly poured. We waited, and the site was destroyed beyond any hope of future use.

The V1/V2 rocket problem remained a high intelligence priority target for the remainder of the war. The V1 "buzz bomb" was mainly targeted against southeastern England and Belgium, while the later V2 rocket had a wider range and a much-increased payload of explosives. We had an intelligence coup on 1 June 1944, just prior to the invasion, when a V2 rocket crash-landed in Sweden. It was later flown to England for Allied analysis. Later, we encountered the V2 operationally. On 8 September 1944 the first German V2 fired in combat exploded in a Paris suburb. A second V2 rocket struck London a few hours later. All told, there were 15 known V2 rocket attacks on the city of Paris. The V2 rockets were launched from mobile platforms because the permanent site at Eperlecques, France, never became operational. The last V2 rocket fired was fired from the Hague on 27 March 1945 against London.

In 1943 we began to receive reports that the German Navy, on Bornholm Island in the Baltic Sea, was attempting to develop a new system to be deployed on its U-boats. The reports stated that the Germans were experimenting with the placement of a "ski-slope" device on the front of their submarines for the firing of rockets. This reporting caused all of the ETOUSA G-2 staff to have great concern for the security of the Eastern seaboard of the United States. German U-boats equipped with the new device could lay off the Eastern seaboard of the U.S. and fire their rockets at U.S. cities.[3] Photographs were eventually taken of the submarines off the coast of Bornholm Island to verify that they actually had a launching ramp on them.

Another "concrete" problem in the arena of technical intelligence that vexed us at ETOUSA headquarters, as well as SHAEF, was the fact that Allied bombs had failed to penetrate the reinforced concrete of German U-boat bins located in Brest, France, since October of 1941. The bins were the home port of the 9th Flotilla, a very potent weapon of the German Navy. For three years, the Allies had been trying to destroy these bins with little luck. Eventually, one of the members of our G-2 staff, a Princeton University physics professor by the name of Dr. H. B. (Bob) Robertson, came up with a solution. He studied all the available photos and other information, and then asked if it could be arranged for an agent to infiltrate the area of the submarine bins at Brest to size the bins and take some specific photographs. Arrangements were accordingly made, and the agent returned with the required data for Dr. Robertson.

Dr. Robertson, working with Dr. R. V. Jones of the U.K., analyzed all the information regarding the structures of the bins. The thickness of the roof was 3.6 meters in the first structure and 4.3 in the last two bins. A second layer of concrete was poured over most of the roof, making the protection 6.2 meters thick. With this information, they calculated exactly where the bombs had to land on the bins to implode them. Allied military personnel developed bombing missions that targeted the bins in August of 1944.[4] We scored nine hits, five of which penetrated, and were delighted with the results. After the war Dr. Robertson would teach at Cal Tech and head a panel that advised then-President Eisenhower on scientific matters. (I was a member of this panel, as well). In my mind, he is one of the unsung heroes of World War II.

German submarine bins at Brest, France. The U-boat bin structure at Brest was 333 meters wide, 192 meters long, and roughly 17 meters high, for a total space of 52,000 square meters. The thickness of the roof was 3.6 meters over bins 1–8 and 4.3 meters over bins 9–10. A second layer of concrete had been poured over the entire roof, making it 6.2 meters thick. The bins were a major base for U-boats operating in the Atlantic Ocean.

Not all technical intelligence was reliable, however; Major Warberg, of the ALSOS team[5], came to me one day and excitedly advised me that he had come across information indicating that the Germans had developed a substance that could serve as a substitute for ball bearings. After that brief encounter, I never heard another word from him about this matter, and to this day, I question what it was he allegedly discovered. Still, the combined result of our technical intelligence activities provided us with information we needed to conduct a successful D-day operation and secure the victory of democracy over the forces of Axis domination.

We at ETOUSA Command maintained an occasional working relationship with the London Office of Strategic Services (OSS), a governmental organization operating out of London and headed in England by Colonel David Bruce. The London OSS was in charge of more sensitive intelligence involving political rather than military affairs. ETOUSA officials believed that such information could prove useful in planning Army tactics and maneuvers, and, consequently, I visited Colonel Bruce to determine what OSS intelligence information

A direct hit by a 12,000-pound Tallboy bomb on the U-boat bins at Brest. Each bomb was 5.4 meters in length. The raids scored nine direct hits and a few near misses. Of the direct hits, five actually penetrated the massive roofs.

should be passed along to new echelons of Army Command. Our new units were just forming at the time, and this question needed to be answered. Bruce said that such information had to be released by the War Department and not by him. OSS intelligence thus was of limited value to ETOUSA throughout the duration of our deployment in Europe. My only other memorable contact with that organization occurred subsequent to the safe return of an OSS agent who had been deliberately dropped behind enemy line in Belgium and who followed a pre-established escape route out of the combat zone. The OSS wanted to award him a Distinguished Service Cross, but I objected, insisting that medals should not be handed out for feats that scores of other airmen had already accomplished with no reward. The agent did not receive a cross. However, it should be noted that OSS intelligence did prove effective in some aspects. In particular, it provided information culled from a close liaison with the French Force of the Interior (FFI) and thereby kept the Allies apprised of goings-on in that Axis-occupied nation. Members of the OSS also worked closely with units in the field and performed meritorious service.

There were various committees operating in England throughout the war, some Allied and some composed strictly of members from one country. I was aware of many of them and cite the following examples of the type of work accomplished by the committees.

First, the American Intelligence Committee (AIC), of which I was a member, was composed of the U.S. ambassador, a U.S. Navy representative, a U.S. Army representative, David Bruce of the London OSS, and other selectees. The committee met regularly to discuss the execution of the war effort and, in particular, the intelligence efforts. This group strongly urged the continual bombing of Europe as a way of ending the war, and they did not believe in the invasion of the continent.

Several studies had been made by this group regarding the possibility of shortening the war through the bombing of the ball-bearing facilities in Germany, which would make impossible the continuation of manufacturing instruments of war such as aircraft, trucks, tanks, and so on. As this study was progressing, it was decided that the targets for the bombing raids would be the elimination of the ball-bearing plants in Schweinfurt and Steyr. Accordingly, the raids were made, at great sacrifice to the Allied effort in the air, as a tremendous number of aircraft were shot down—but the facilities manufacturing ball bearings appeared to be eliminated.

Colonel David Bruce, Chief, Office of Strategic Services, Europe, 1943.

General William Donovan, Chief OSS, and Colonel Ralph W. Hauenstein. This photo was taken in Grand Rapids, Michigan, after the close of the war, 1945.

In the ensuing months, the Germans did not seem to be held up in any of their manufacturing of the tools of war. Further study revealed that Sweden was providing the necessary supply that had been eliminated in Germany. Using diplomatic channels, Washington sent a representative to meet with government officials there and urged that they discontinue the shipments to Germany. Sweden asked for time to consider, but in a very short period, Swedish officials replied that since Germany had been their number one trading partner for many, many years, they could not accede to the request. Sweden was then advised that if it continued such shipments, it would be placed on the "black list" by America for all types of trading. Again, Sweden asked for time to consider, then came back with a negative reply. This decision was followed by a third meeting at which Sweden was advised that SKF (Svenska Kullagerfabriken; a manufacturer of ball bearings) holdings in America and other key interests would be confiscated if such acts continued. Once again, Sweden rejected the request and continued the ball-bearing shipments to Germany.

A final statement was then made to Sweden in appreciation for allowing damaged U.S. planes returning from German bombing raids to land safely in Sweden. America did appreciate this, but it was advised that because ball-bearing factories may look very similar in Sweden as they do in Germany, American planes might unfortunately bomb the plants by mistake. At that point, Sweden discontinued its shipments to Germany. In the meantime, the Germans had disbursed manufacturing to small factory units throughout Germany, and they were able to make up the major part of the requirements for ball bearings that had been lost through our bombings.

Second, I was aware that the British had a small elite group of individuals (some military and some civilian) who developed the deception plans used by the Allies during the course of the war. They were known as the "London Controlling Section" (L.C.S.), and were never fully publicly identified. Among their triumphs were the phantom Army units of General George Patton's 1st U.S. Army Group (FUSAG) in the south of England, the Army in northern England and the troops in Iceland and Scotland purported to be there to invade Norway, and the body that washed ashore in Spain carrying documentation on the invasion of Greece. The members of this group were never identified nor officially named. You saw the results of their devious planning, but you never saw them.

The cover names associated with the various deception plans were:

BODYGUARD: Deception planning for Northeast Europe

FORTITUDE: Deception planning to protect the NEPTUNE (assault Phase of OVERLORD). There were two separate FORTITUDE operations, FORTITUDE NORTH and FORTITUDE SOUTH

Third, along with the general deception plan, there was a group called the Twenty Committee, a subset of the W. Board that consisted of the three directors of intelligence plus MI6 and MI5 (known as the Group of 5). The group was named the Twenty Committee, as the Roman numeral for twenty, XX, is also the sign for a double cross. It was tasked to "turn" the captured German agents who had infiltrated Allied countries (particularly England and Iceland) and have them send misinformation back to their German handlers on the continent. The program was extremely successful from early 1941 until the end of the war. They also worked through the two double agents we had in Iceland, COBWEB and BEETLE.

Once the Allied forces were in place on the continent, both the deception and double-cross programs were expanded and operated within the Army groups. I was aware of the fact that the 21st Army Group (Northern) and the 12th Army Group (Southern) formed a committee for deception and called it the 212 Committee (21 for the Northern Armies and 12 for the Southern Armies). The committee's main role was to continue existing deception tactics against the Nazi forces and continue to "turn" German agents caught as the troops advanced.

All the activities of the intelligence committees and groups depended on strict maintenance of tight security. The phrase "need-to-know" became part of every intelligence officer's vocabulary.

Prior to the invasion, the emphasis on security was extremely tight, particularly regarding the activities of the troops stationed in England, but, we did have our lapses. One good example was the planned practice invasion exercise known as Operation TIGER, which was to take place at Slapton Sands on the southern coast of England. Our intelligence operations failed to provide any advance intelligence regarding the threat of German submarine attacks during the exercise.[6] That experience served to make us work harder at providing critical intelligence.

Another major project was Operation CARPETBAGGER, which was the cover name for the U.K. efforts to send supplies to underground units on the continent. The airborne effort commenced on 4 January 1944 and continued until late September 1944. The underground units operating in Europe had become an essential part of our overall intelligence network; our success or failure on D-day depended on good information from all of these sources, particularly the French Resistance. We had almost lost the French Resistance during the North African campaign over the Allied use of Admiral Jean-Francois Darlan to sway the French in North Africa. Although French, he was a known Nazi sympathizer, which caused the French Resistance to "go to ground" (reduce activity levels) rather than have him learn of their work through the Allies, and then report it to the Nazis. The French were a very important source of intelligence to us, and great efforts were made to restore their confidence in the efforts of the Allies on their behalf.

Our relations with the military missions of Belgium, France, Netherlands, and Norway, all areas of specific interest to SHAEF's future actions on the continent, increased during the pre-invasion period. On 25 May 1944, the missions of these countries were asked to provide officers to be assigned to units that would be entering their countries. These officers were to advise the Allied military authorities in administrative functions, intelligence, plans and operations, civil affairs, and psychological warfare pertaining to their specific country. The Belgians, the Dutch, and the Norwegians all agreed to the assignment and acted accordingly. The French, in the form of Charles DeGaulle, presented a unique problem. It was not until two days before the scheduled invasion of Europe that the French agreed to supply the requested advisors.

I was privy to all manner of discreet information, none more so than top-secret German messages cracked by code breakers at Bletchley Park. When I was initially briefed on ULTRA, the code word used to designate ENIGMA-decrypted messages, I was astounded at what I learned. On a regular basis, the crew at Bletchley had succeeded in reading the messages encoded in what the Germans believed to be an unbreakable cipher machine named ENIGMA. At that time it represented a very complex machine. The British had fallen heir to an ENIGMA machine, and some of the initial breaking techniques employed by a group of Polish mathematicians prior to the fall of Poland. All of the German services, including their army, navy, air force, and Gestapo, used the ENIGMA, so the decrypted messages were a very valuable source of intelligence. The Bletchley output was shared only with U.S. intelligence—none of the other Allies—and, indeed, proved invaluable (sometimes, almost too good). Senior officials came to rely so heavily on Bletchley Park's output that if information was not in the ENIGMA traffic, it was not considered reliable. One good example of problems that caused was the attack known as the "Bulge," which was difficult to predict because of German radio silence in the area—there were no ENIGMA messages to tip their hand.

The ULTRA material we received in ETOUSA was normally in report format and not complete translations of the original message. The report might be based on one message or on a collection of related material. It was timely, accurate, and relative to the current situation. While we had the authority to query Bletchley Park regarding either a report or any other questions for which we thought they might have the answer, that was rarely done; their reporting filled the bill.

At the same time we also received, from American code breakers, the diplomatic traffic that flowed from Japanese ambassadors around the world back to Tokyo. This traffic was nicknamed MAGIC (by the U.K.), and it was. The Japanese ambassador in Berlin, a man named Baron Hiroshi Oshima, was a close personal friend of Hitler and met with him regularly. The results of these meetings were transmitted by Oshima to Tokyo in MAGIC, and it was not unusual for us to have the decrypt before Tokyo had received it. One example of Oshima's value is that, prior to D-day, he had taken a tour of the defenses along the French coast and very carefully reported his observations back to his capital. We protected the security of these highly sensitive messages with utmost care. Wonderful stuff.

While ETOUSA G-2 received ULTRA reports, the U.S. Army units being formed at that time did not. This posed a serious problem—how do we get the information to the forces that require it and, at the same time, protect the source of the material? On 15 March 1944, General Marshall sent General Eisenhower a letter that set out the basis upon which German ULTRA intelligence was to be passed on to the U.S. Army field commands. That letter was given to ETOUSA G-2 for implementation. The letter stated that:

- The receipt and distribution at the field commands of ULTRA messages was to be handled by special liaison units (SLU) furnished and controlled by the director general G.C. and C.S. (Government Codes and Cipher School, U.K.). The personnel of these units included American officers attached to MID, War Department, London.

- One or more American officers would be assigned to each SLU normally commanded by a U.K. officer, although several SLUs were, in fact, commanded by U.S Army officers.

- All the SLUs were controlled by SLU 9 at SHAEF and were attached to U.S. field commands.

- All the personnel were trained at Bletchley Park prior to being assigned to a specific unit.

- Deliveries were made to the command normally four times a day.

In total, 28 U.S. officers served, at one time or another, as ULTRA representatives in the European Theater. Of these, only two were regular Army officers with military experience; the rest were reserve officers. By far the largest group selected to serve with the SLUs had been lawyers in civilian life, but the list included teachers, reporters, an engineer, and a corporate executive. All were functioning with their units prior to D-day and went into action with the invasion. Colonel Telford Taylor was director of the American ULTRA program in Europe.

The newly assigned G-2 branch chief of ETOUSA, Brigadier General Edmund Sibert, a man of whom my initial impressions were not favorable, appeared on the scene. I perceived General Sibert as being more concerned about external appearances than about the hard and fast realities of military life. For instance, as his first directive to a group meeting during which he was introduced to his officers, he made the comment that there was too much fraternization with enlisted personnel outside of headquarters, and we must eliminate such fraternization immediately. Sibert was not at our command long, however, so this edict did not become an issue. The glamour of life in the field appealed to him more than did life at a desk in headquarters, and he eventually became G-2 of the 12th Army Group.

The group charged with the planning efforts for the invasion of Europe was called the Committee of Twenty (not to be confused with the Twenty Committee). The proposed invasion plans for invading the continent were finalized in December of 1943, just prior to the arrival of General Eisenhower as commanding general. Once he arrived in January of 1944, the wheels of motion began. Having been a part of Operation RATTLE, the planning for OVERLORD, I knew basically the plan presented to General Eisenhower. General Eisenhower basically knew the outline of the plan, as he had developed it initially when he served as the assistant chief of staff, U.S. Army, but now he had to approve it in its final form.

On 21 January 1944 Eisenhower held a major meeting with the OVERLORD staff to discuss it in detail. We all awaited the outcome of that session. Necessary changes were made, and in February of 1944 General Eisenhower was given the go-ahead to invade the continent. Now our work really began in earnest. But it was not until 8 May 1944 that we knew the actual planned date for the invasion. That date was 5 June 1944.

Prior to the initiation of Project OVERLORD, daily life of the intelligence staffs of SHAEF and ETOUSA was filled with tension and apprehension. We worried that some little detail or major turn of events would disrupt all our well-developed plans. By late May 1944, we thought we had the intelligence structure of the troops established, and qualified military intelligence officers in place, with a good understanding of their specific roles in support of the troops. We were confident that we had done our job. But I kept remembering a briefing I had received early in 1944, one I still remember as vividly as if it were yesterday. It was in regard to the German nuclear program. Would this affect our endeavors?

The potential of German development of nuclear devices had always been high on our intelligence collection list. We in Europe were charged with developing intelligence on the German capabilities, and we did our job. For example, when we learned that a heavy water facility in Norway was a potential reservoir for the generation of German atomic power, we immediately eliminated it. Job well done. However, there was another potential threat that worried the scientists in the MANHATTAN Project—that of radiation poisoning. That risk had the potential to disrupt all our planning and could possibly change the course of warfare. In January of 1944, a U.S. Army major by the name of Horace K. (Tony) Calvert appeared in my office. He had just been assigned to London to open a MANHATTAN Project liaison office to serve as a point of contact with British intelligence, as well as the G-2 of ETOUSA. Prior to his arrival, I had never heard of the MANHATTAN Project.

His initial orders were to brief the commanding general and the G-2 of ETOUSA. However, in early January of 1944, there was no commanding general of ETOUSA. General Devers was on his way to relieve General Eisenhower in Africa. And Eisenhower, in turn, was returning to England to assume command of ETOUSA. When Major Calvert approached General David G. Barr, the Deputy of ETOUSA, he was quickly sent to the G-2 of ETOUSA, Colonel Bryan Conrad, who, in turn, sent him on to me as the chief of the G-2 intelligence staff.

Major Calvert handed me a very short letter signed by Secretary of War Stimpson. It advised that Calvert would brief the commander of ETOUSA, as well as the proper intelligence structure, on the development of an atomic weapon being conducted by Project MAN-HATTAN. Major Calvert brought me up to date on the MANHATTAN Project. He informed me that the U.S. was about to conduct an atom-splitting chain reaction. The chilling part came when he stated that they were not entirely sure that the chain reaction could be stopped!

Later, in April of 1944, I learned that the MANHATTAN Project scientists, while certain that the German development of a nuclear capability was virtually nonexistent, were still concerned about the possibility of the use of radiation in the tactical environment. A project code-named Operation PEPPERMINT had been mounted to alert all Army commands about the potential dangers of radiation poisoning. Major Calvert sought to have the troops in the field alerted to report back immediately if they saw a purple-colored cloud in the sky, if they encountered blue smoke, or if they noted any photographic film that could not be developed after a photograph had been taken. No reason was to be given to the troops for the alert. A similar alert had been given to the U.K. for its troops. It was a moment I will never forget!

Major Calvert advised me that the senior commanders would also be told about Operation PEPPERMINT, but I was sworn to secrecy and warned not to discuss any of the information with any other officer. With all of our other responsibilities at the time, this was an awesome task to undertake—but it was done.

I was also told that a Colonel Boris Pash, chief of the ALSOS mission in Italy, would be coming to establish a similar unit in the European Theater and that his reports would be forwarded to American authorities through my office. The MANHATTAN Project wanted a group to be with the American forces as they advanced, first in Italy and then in Europe. The group would be composed of specialists in nuclear science, and they would be looking for evidence of nuclear development as the American troops advanced. The group was code named ALSOS, which happens to be the Greek word for "grove," a play on words as the head of the MANHATTAN Project was a General Leslie M. Groves.

As the date for D-day approached, all eyes were, of course, on the weather. If it continued to deteriorate, and the invasion was made impossible, all bets were off. The weather broke, and D-day became a reality for all of us.

As our troops prepared to land on the coast of France, we felt that our intelligence efforts had provided them with a substantial amount of intelligence on the German forces they were about to meet. We knew that:

- Many of the German divisions facing the Allied forces were woefully understaffed; for example, a German division's authorized strength was 15,000 men, and many along the coast of France had fewer than 10,000.

- Many of the German soldiers were, in fact, Hitler Youths with virtually no combat experience.

- There was a severe fuel shortage in France for the German vehicles.

- Our maps indicated the deployment of the German units all along the French coast were based on information supplied by the FFI (French Forces of the Interior); these maps proved to be a very accurate depiction of the German forces facing our invading force.

We also knew that deception plans suggesting that we planned an invasion in the Calais area were working. Specifically, through ENIGMA decrypts, we knew that the 116th Panzer Tank Division was being held in the Calais area and that it was under the direct control of Hitler himself.

Prior to the invasion, the real value of the FFI, known to us as the French Resistance, came to the fore. Their guerrillas blew up bridges and railroad tracks and blocked major roads. They greatly hampered the ability of the German army to move its forces.

All of this information had been given to the Allied Commands prior to their landing on the continent. We had done our job—not as

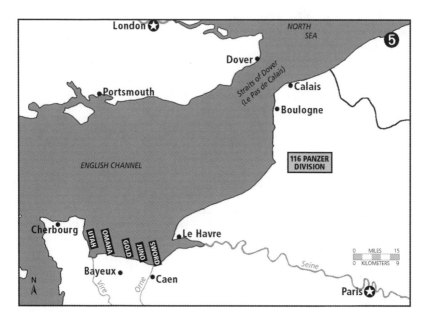

Allied D-Day invasion beaches. The five Allied invasion beaches in France were south of the Calais area where the Germans expected the invasion to take place. The 116th Panzer Division's position in the Calais area was a definite asset for the success of the Allied invasion.

completely as we would have liked, but we felt we had done our job in support of our troops.

The intelligence staff also knew that unless the German ENIGMA traffic was compromised or changed, we would continue to read it, allowing us to supply daily valuable tactical intelligence to our troops. We also hoped that the diplomatic reports of Baron Oshima from Berlin to Tokyo would continue to supply us with high-level intelligence regarding Hitler and his high command. Our concern was not to let anyone know how much we knew or how we gained the knowledge.

Post D-day, we all exhaled. Our intelligence had provided the necessary tactical information to the Allied troops, and both the German ENIGMA and the Japanese PURPLE (MAGIC to the U.K.) traffic continued to flow from the Axis powers.

NOTES

1. During the war years, there were about 436 Americans involved with the British in both the collection and breaking of the ENIGMA traffic. They were designated as the Signal Corps, 6811th, 6812th and, 6813th Detachments—subordinate to ETOUSA, but with a mission unknown to most of the ETOUSA staff members. The 6811th was at Blexley, Kent where they manned an intercept site, the 6812th was located at Eastcote near Harrow working on the "bombes" and the 6813th worked directly with the U.K. at Bletchley. The entire effort was code named BEECHNUT.

2. The bombing of the Peenemuende area in August of 1943 (Operation CROSSBOW) is estimated to have delayed German rocket development for at least six months. The raid was comprised of over 570 bombers with 2,000 tons of bombs.

3. As early as 1943, the German Navy experimented in the Baltic Sea with firing a rocket from a submarine. It proved to be ineffective and difficult. There were no further reports of such a development for a German U-boat.

4. The RAF had been bombing the submarine base since January of 1941 with very limited success. They were joined by the USAAF in January 1943, and together they flew over 80 missions in a futile effort to damage the bins. The bombing raids based on Dr. Robertson's analysis for ETOUSA (G-2) were conducted on 8, 12 and 13 August 1944 by the 617th RAF Squadron.

5. ALSOS was the cover name for MANHATTAN Project personnel operating in Europe. The word ALSOS is Greek for Grove, and the MANHATTAN Project was headed by General Leslie M. Groves.

6. On 26 April 1944 Operation TIGER was conducted at Slapton Sands, as an exercise for the invasion at Normandy. Nine German U-boats entered the area and sank two LSTs and damaged a third. The total loss of American life was 97 sailors and 441 soldiers.

The British

My first reactions to the British were not particularly positive. I found them to be stuffy, and in my specific world of intelligence, they felt that they were the supreme authorities on the subject—and in many ways they were. We had a lot to learn, and I must admit they accommodated our needs—at least most of them! I maintained a close working relationship with British intelligence officers during my deployment in Iceland and London, as well as personal relationships with several British civilians. The better I got to know the British, both professionally and personally, the more my first impressions proved to be wrong.

My feelings began to change favorably as I shared their hours of turmoil during the German bombings of London and other cities. The raids began in 1940 and 1941, long before I arrived in England, and continued until late in the war years in an attempt to destroy morale and force Britain's surrender. I did not experience the air war over Britain, which occurred before I arrived, but I did experience the rocket attacks. On 13 June 1944 the Germans began dropping the V1 rockets on London. Between 13 June and 20 June, over 8,000 were launched against England. Later, on 15 September 1944, the V2 rockets began to fall on London. At least 1,000 V2s were targeted against London. The stoicism with which the British handled this horrible onslaught was an inspiration to me.

One evening I was near Piccadilly Square when air raid sirens began to sound. Like all good Londoners, I headed to a subway station—the tube—for safety. The station was so packed with people that I could not even move my shoulders, but it afforded protection from the cacophony overhead—or so we thought. Suddenly, a bomb crashed through the tunnel just beyond the platform, spewing dust, debris, and chunks of concrete in all directions. The noise was deafening, but the crowd remained perfectly still, letting no sound emanate, and since there were no casualties that required attention, the people remained that way for almost an hour after the blast. My admiration for the strength with which these people handled that experience persists and influences the way I perceive them to this very day.

As more and more American troops arrived in the United Kingdom, my respect for the British continued to grow. In early 1942 that tiny island nation had been host to about 5,000 U.S. Army personnel located in various areas of the U.K. By mid-1944, just prior to the invasion, it had welcomed 1.5 million U.S. GIs. Their small island nation, in many ways isolated from the rest of Europe, was suddenly inundated with literally millions of American young men and women. Some Britishers were heard to remark that England had become the United States' biggest aircraft carrier.

Billeting of the American troops soon became a problem. British families in many areas were informed that if they had a spare bedroom, they would be billeting American troops—they needn't volunteer; soldiers would just arrive. The upside of this was that American boarders came with American rations, which were a welcome payment for the British who were under severe rationing at the time. The British accepted this move with very little resentment; their future freedom depended on their full cooperation and support.

In addition to the influx of American military men and women, the U.K. was also flooded with American equipment. On 31 January 1942 there had been 881,554 long tons of American equipment and supplies stored on U.K. soil. By 31 January 1944 that total had increased nearly four times, to 3,497,761, and just prior to the invasion it peaked at 5,297,306 long tons.

To add further inconvenience for the locals, for a period of time prior to the invasion, a large section of southeastern England was under quarantine. No one left the area, and no unauthorized person was allowed into the area.

While on duty in London, I felt some uneasiness when it came to being an American there. Londoners were like the rest of England, under strict rationing, with very few options for food. I, in contrast, had access to the American mess arrangements, providing food from the United States not governed by British rationing. We could not expect the British to feed the ever-increasing number of Americans. Periodically, I would take a British officer for a meal in our mess but did not do it frequently, in part because I worried that the dramatic

Rosa Lewis, ex-chef to royalty and charismatic owner of the Cavendish House Hotel, a haven for both U.S. and British officers during the blitz of England. Affectionately known as the Duchess of Jermyn Street.

differences between the average English diet and the American military diet would cause resentment. I do believe that the British realized that there was no way they could feed millions of newcomers to their country with their limited food supplies, and therefore they appreciated the American efforts not to deplete their food supply. But how they felt about our unwillingness to share, I dare not guess.

Not all Brits I met were the embodiment of stoicism and reserve. Perhaps the liveliest person I encountered in London was a lady by the name of Rosa Lewis, owner of the Cavendish House Hotel. I lived near this establishment and occasionally stopped in for drinks after attending a play or enduring a late night at work. She owned the hotel and had a reputation for refusing guests she did not enjoy. I feel—and still feel—honored that she approved of my presence in her pub.

Mrs. Lewis in her youth had been a very attractive girl and had become quite a good cook. She grew very popular with the aristocratic set in London and was a favorite cook to Prince Edward VII, the

Cavendish House Hotel, London, owned and operated by Rosa Lewis.

crown prince. It was also rumored that she became one of his mistresses and, in fact, that he had presented her with the hotel property, as he had done to other mistresses, as a token of his appreciation (the hotel grant, at least in her case, was not true). By World War II, she was in her eighties, and her beauty had somewhat faded, but her dynamic personality remained intact. I would describe her manner of dress as less than tidy, and her hair often looked as though a bird had found a happy nesting place above her still-enchanting countenance. On one occasion, we were sitting together enjoying a whiskey, when a British admiral arrived. With furrowed brow and not too quiet a voice, Mrs. Lewis declared, "Oh God, here comes that wet dream." The remark was typically Rosa.

The Cavendish House Hotel later came under fire during a German air raid, and Rosa sustained injuries that required hospitalization. Lying on a stretcher, she still found enough strength to give orders to her staff. She demanded that they continue operations, regardless of damages to the hotel or to the lady who owned it. She soon returned, bandages and all, to reign once more.

When Rosa died on 28 November 1952 her coffin bore wreaths from the Queen Mother's brother, the Marquess and Marchioness of Bath, the Earl of Sandwich, and others. I had been told many stories about Rosa—the mistress of a king, a charmer of nobility, and a friend of the affluent—but to me she had been an absolute jewel in this hellish war with its daily bombings and its tortured souls.

Role of G-2 ETOUSA in the Early Campaign in Europe

As the date for the invasion of Europe drew nearer, General Eisenhower and several members of his staff established a temporary headquarters for the Allied command at Portsmouth, on the southern coast of England, because of that location's proximity to the shores of Normandy. The area was in what we called a virtual state of quarantine preceding the actual invasion. No one left the area, and only essential personnel were allowed to enter—it was in effect a lockdown.

A small cadre of staff officers accompanied Ike's staff, but I remained at the headquarters in London, monitoring the current situation from our headquarters at 20 Grosvenor Square. This was the time for the intelligence officers we had been training in England to show their worth. While I knew we had trained a competent group of tactical intelligence officers, there was still some personal apprehension as to how they would function in an actual war environment. From the very onset, it was apparent that the training was paying off in a grand manner. So it now became my role to assist them from a distance. I was involved daily in various intelligence matters that impacted on all the U.S. forces, not just one specific command. My staff remained in London even after 7 August 1944 when Eisenhower moved his forward headquarters to Normandy (the same day as the German counteroffensive began at Motrain). A forward element of ETOUSA went with him. Though I was in Normandy and other points in France much earlier, it was not until September of 1944 that a full complement of ETOUSA G-2 operations rejoined our fellow troops on the continent.

My first personal encounter with General Eisenhower had been in London, and I found him a pleasant man, easy to work with, as well as demanding. All of his leadership qualities, along with his demeanor and interest in his troops, made him the perfect choice to

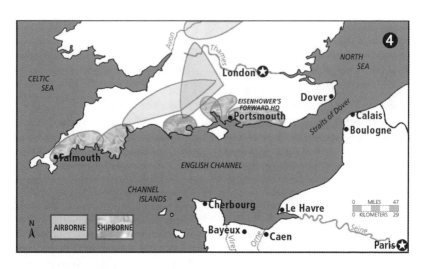

Predeployment troop locations. The area of England south of London was virtually one big military camp prior to D-day. Troops were quartered as far east as Falmouth and all along the southern coastline. General Eisenhower moved his forward headquarters to Portsmouth to be in closer proximity to the troops.

serve as head of the Allied Command, since he was able to achieve cooperation and coordination among disparate armed forces and nations typically not used to working together—and especially with an American in charge! The stunning victory the Allies achieved on the shores of Normandy and their rapid spread over the European continent pays testament to the strength of General Eisenhower's military capability.

The G-2 ETOUSA intelligence activity, however, did not stop once the invasion had taken place, and our military intelligence officers began to support the various U.S. units. In fact, our activity became all the more important as our role was shifting. The intelligence trainees were now serving with combat units and supporting their intelligence requirements, and they would continue to do so for the remainder of the war. We would provide assistance: they were the forward edge to combat units for intelligence; in contrast, we had a secondary mission to perform—that of base sectors.

Base sectors had to be established that would maintain responsibility for the management of a particular area once it was freed from the German occupation. Each sector was to be headed by a brigadier general and presided over by his staff. It was my duty to brief the G-2s from each sector on the procedures they should follow in conducting intelligence operations in their specific sectors. These operations were to be directed against the Germans who may have left behind agents, guerrillas, and the like. The sectors were to ensure that no trouble arose behind the U.S. Army lines that would cause a distraction for current operations. This particular function of ETOUSA is one of the major roles of ETOUSA (G-2) that is frequently overlooked by World War II historians—it was not particularly glamorous.

Our role in the G-2 of ETOUSA shifted after the invasion of Europe. In addition to the base sectors, we also had the responsibility of servicing the requirements that transcended a particular Army and that affected all U.S. Army commands. We were tasked, in addition, with meeting the intelligence requirements of the Services of Supply elements (COM Z), servicing the advancing American troops. One advantage that we had in the G-2 ETOUSA was that we could anticipate intelligence requirements, as we were in an "overview" position, and with a little initiative, quick responses became a norm for us.

All of the intelligence we derived was coordinated with SHAEF, with few exceptions. Certain reports relating to German efforts on nuclear fusion (code-named ALSOS) and the counterintelligence area

(CIC, or Counter Intelligence Corps) were held within U.S. channels only. They were made available upon request by various units of the U.S. Army, if the request was deemed to be warranted.

Our intelligence structure throughout the war period could best be described as a work in progress. As new requirements arose, shifts were made in our overall structure. The overall SHAEF intelligence structure can best be explained as follows. The major intelligence services available to the supreme commander, Allied Expeditionary Force, and very familiar to me were of two types:

1. Intelligence services of the major commanders:
   - 6th, 12th, and 21st Army Groups
   - 1st British Tactical AF, 9th USAF, and 1st U.S. Tactical
   - Allied Naval Continental Expeditionary Force
   - Hq., ETOUSA
   - Hq., U.S. Strategic Air Force
   - Hq., commander of the Navy in Europe

2. Intelligence services from outside agencies
   - U.S. departments and agencies
   - UK ministries and agencies

In addition, there were several committees in which we, the G-2 ETOUSA, were occasionally involved. They were:

3. The Joint Intelligence Committee, which was formed in order to provide the supreme commander, SHAEF, with coordinated air, ground, and naval intelligence. It was composed of U.S. and U.K. staff members from the ground, air, and naval areas of operation.

4. The Combined Strategic Targets Committee served as an advisory committee that met for the purpose of establishing priorities of targets to be attacked by the Allied air forces. Industrialists, as well as representatives of the staffs of the major commands in Europe, were members of the committee. This committee frequently used the G-2 intelligence staff of ETOUSA as a resource pool.

In addition to the above, there were specific elements within the G-2 ETOUSA organization that proved very effective in our role of intelligence gathering and interpretation during the war years. First was my organization, the G-2 Intelligence Branch, which supplied intelligence up and down the chain of command.

On the tactical level of ETOUSA, the U.S. Army Groups, once activated, had their own intelligence organizations. These intelligence staffs were the primary source of intelligence derived from tactical operations in the European Theater of Operations. Their reports were forwarded through the regular channels to SHAEF, to other commands, and to G-2, ETOUSA, on a need-to-know basis.

All of the above briefly describes the U.S. intelligence network that was alive and functioning almost immediately upon the arrival of U.S. ground forces in Europe. And in spite of the apparently complex structure, all of us working within the system managed their portion, admirably. The job was accomplished.

From the hands-on point of view, we quickly put the new structure in effect. We knew that the Germans were hungry for revenge to counter our invasion of France. Therefore, we knew that we needed to maintain a vigilant watch over them to ensure that any counteroffensive measure they attempted would not be successful. We received an opportunity to test the efficacy of our ULTRA interpretation system very quickly when we received messages (via the British code-breaking effort at Bletchley Park) that a cadre of Germans on the Channel Islands was preparing to attack the French coast. The cadre was small, but it had confiscated fishing boats belonging to French islanders and was gathering resources for a surprise assault on the mainland to be held at a later date. Since this was an ULTRA factor, I did not wish it to be relayed by any other manner than by a personal visit. Accordingly, I visited the G-2 of the area and personally gave him the story that we had a reconnaissance flight over the Channel Islands and discovered that the Germans were outfitting confiscated fishing boats and equipping them for landings. A later flight showed that they were preparing themselves by making various types of assaults on the island coasts preparatory for such an attack. With all of this information, it was obvious that, for his area, the responsible G-2 needed to be prepared for an assault in the coming days or weeks. This was sufficient, in my opinion, to warrant extra guarding along the coast, and I so warned him. However, he did not take the warning sufficiently serious and took no safeguards whatsoever. The attack came some days later and was successful. The incident was even more notable because as a result of the assault the Germans had captured a Red Cross nurse who was an acquaintance of General Eisenhower. The general demanded a full accounting of the incident and, fortunately, after diplomatic negotiations, was able to secure the nurse's release. It was an early lesson learned for our new intelligence officers.

About this time, we in the ETOUSA G-2 viewed a disturbing German propaganda film. It depicted the reception American troops captured during the D-day invasion had received from the French as they were paraded down the Champs-Elysées shortly after their apprehension. These soldiers were spat on, hit, and harassed by Parisians, who had quickly defected from the Allies back to their German occupiers. It was a heartbreaking sight, one that solidified our resolve to eliminate the Axis powers inflicting such humiliation. The film did not help the cause of the French after their liberation.

Because the need for mobility in gathering intelligence after the D-day invasion was a real one, collection of intelligence data was paramount. On 17 June 1944, I was issued a special identification card that allowed me virtual carte blanche authority to carry out my duties as I desired throughout the Allied occupied zones. I could photograph at will, interrogate prisoners and refugees, examine and remove enemy equipment, and take whatever measures were necessary to thwart espionage or sabotage against our forces.

It was a card that I put to good use in the execution of my responsibilities, and, it even led to a rather "testy" encounter with the famed General George S. Patton. I had come upon his jeep one cold winter day and had been questioned by his aide as to my use of a vehicle with side curtains, since the general had expressly prohibited use of these curtains in command cars and jeeps. I presented my ID card, which General Patton's aide examined, and was directed by the general through his men to proceed on. I could see from the expression on Patton's face that he was not pleased. He was not accustomed to being countermanded by a mere colonel. However, on other occasions when I saw him, he was quite amiable.

I well remember when General Lesley McNair was killed in battle on 25 July 1944. His death was the result of friendly fire. General McNair, a War Department observer, was accredited as commanding general of the U.S. 1st Army, which was only a paper organization. This paper Army was part of the master deception plan to confuse the Germans, and it worked. The death of General McNair was a definite

Colonel Hauenstein's special pass for traveling and military business, issued by General Dwight D. Eisenhower.

loss to the Allied combat efforts. General McNair was the highest-ranking U.S. Army officer killed in the European Theater during World War II.

From the very onset of the invasion of Europe, the "biggest nut to crack" for intelligence personnel was the constant problem of Order of Battle (OB). All of the subordinate G-2s supplied us with a variety of intelligence reports to include Intelligence Summaries (ISUM; two times weekly), G-2 Periodic Reports (every 24 hours), Weekly Supplements to Periodic Reports, Estimates of Situation, as well as other reports as required. All of the unit intelligence sources were supplemented by other sources—ULTRA, prisoners of war, agents, FFI, aerial photos, and expert OB teams—yet we still could not always be completely accurate in locating enemy formations. The Battle of the Bulge was to become a prime example of this problem.

My personal assessment of German intelligence is that their best intelligence was our own information that we gave to them. They did not follow up on their ideas and analysis with exploratory efforts (i.e., photo, spies, or submarine observations). For example, the 55th Infantry Division in Iceland (a phantom division) was rumored to be on tap to invade Norway. This unit was purely fictitious—existing only on paper. The Germans never ascertained this fact, as they did no missions to gather the data. They merely accepted the reports from German double agents under our direction and acted accordingly, as they did on numerous occasions, especially during the time period of the invasion of France.

Paris

August 1944 to May 1945

The Allies had been marching through Europe with Paris on their minds, and they began their liberation of this city on 23 August 1944. From my base in Normandy, we received confirmation that the Germans were departing, and plans were resolved that official liberation duties should be handed over to the French 2nd Armored Division, led by Brigadier General Jacques-Philippe LeClerc. However, it was decided that America needed an immediate presence in the newly liberated city as well, and consequently I was ordered to proceed to the French capital, where I became one of the first American military men to enter Paris after the fall of the Nazis. Later I learned that the author Ernest Hemingway, accompanied by an OSS officer, had circumvented the chain of command and arrived in Paris at approximately the same time; another general, chief of the Signal Corps, also made his way to the city about the same time, for purposes of securing signal connections.

Following the Paris discussions in an orchard of a distant suburban Paris (attended by Generals Bradley, Patton, and Walker), I left for Paris. After some discussion, it was understood that the French should be the first to enter the city officially.

As an indication of the camaraderie that existed between the American high command, let me relate the following incident. As the meeting in the orchard was breaking up, I turned to leave. General Bradley, who had been a star baseball pitcher at West Point, picked up an apple and pitched a nice curve ball, hitting me on the rear end! Later, using my special pass, I commandeered an L5 observation plane to make the trip. My heart was pounding with anticipation as the young pilot transported me there. We took turns observing and flying as we glided over the French countryside. Using a railroad track as a point of identification, we flew into suburban Paris and chose to land on a small football field. Immediately after landing, we realized the field was too small to attempt a takeoff, but before we could resolve this problem, the FFI arrived in vehicles displaying the tricolors with an enthusiastic and long-awaited greeting. One man spoke broken English and, upon learning that we were Americans, greeted us in a typically affectionate French manner (which found little favor with this staid Midwesterner).

The French drove me into Paris in what would become one of the most frightening trips of my life. With horns blasting, tires spinning, pedestrians jumping out of death's way, we sped toward the heart of the city. Explosions kept resounding as though we were being struck by enemy fire, but my new FFI friends paid no mind to the cacophony. I knew that several hundred Germans remained in the city, and I feared they might be showing violent displeasure at the change of the guard. Noticing my alarm, the French informed me that the vehicle's charcoal-burning engine was the cause of the noise—not German saboteurs, as I had surmised. Still this news did little to assuage my fears on the chaotic car ride.

The French deposited me first at the Majestic Hotel, which had served as the headquarters for the German high command, and then at the Hotel George V, after we found the former hotel deserted. The entire staff of the hotel was standing at full attention, ready to welcome the Allies as replacements for the German general staff they had previously served so graciously. I took up residence in the former quarters of Field Marshal Gerd von Rundstedt, commander of the German forces on the Western Front, to rest and to soak up the sights and sounds of the heady excitement that followed the Allied occupation. In one room of von Rundstedt's office, I found a stock of wine, cognac, and champagne.

My first indication that things were returning to normal occurred the next day. I was sitting in Hotel George V's bar when two men walked in sporting American officers' uniforms but lacking any insignia. I asked who they were, and they quickly produced letters of identification from Washington stating they were representatives of Coca-Cola whose mission was to activate the production of this popular soft drink as soon as possible. They had been given the status of "technical advisors" to facilitate such a morale booster. It was then that I knew a change of guard had truly taken place.[1] I vacated my comfortable quarters shortly thereafter.

During those early days in Paris, I was in frequent contact with the FFI. My main contact was a man then known as Colonel Rémy, who was the head of an FFI group known as Confrere de Notre Dame. Early in the war, he and his family had been secreted out of France to avoid the Gestapo's arresting him. He was now back in France as a member of the de Gaulle group and doing great work. Colonel Rémy worked closely with another Frenchman named Colonel Pol, also a member of the FFI. I later learned that Colonel Rémy's real name was Gilbert Renault-Roulier, the French writer, and his associate, was in fact, a man named Roger Dumant. Both did excellent intelligence work and were very helpful to American intelligence efforts.

In 1954, I had reason to correspond with Renault-Roulier on a business matter, and I asked him about his "Rémy identity." The reply is quoted below:

Lisbon
14 November 1954

Colonel Ralph W. Hauenstein
60 East 42nd Street
NY, NY

My Dear Colonel:

* * *

Regarding my identity there is no doubt in the eyes of the law that I am Gilbert Renault. But some have taken the habit of calling me Colonel Rémy which the law itself doesn't worry about. I am reconciled by my part by signing Gilbert Renault sed Rémy.

Very cordially yours.

Gilbert Renault sed Rémy

As I interacted with Parisians in those first few days after the Allied liberation, I found that many of the residents of Paris were most anxious to prove to the Allied Forces that they were not Nazi collaborators, but, in fact, supported the Allied cause. One name that immediately comes to mind is Maurice Chevalier, who had entertained the German military in Paris. Another one that comes to mind

117

was George Carpentier, a former boxing champion who had been defeated by Jack Dempsey in a world title fight and who now worked as the quasi manager at the famous cafe in Paris called La Lido.

Mr. Carpentier sought me out and invited me to accompany him to a show at his establishment. I accepted the invitation and, when we arrived at the Lido on the Champs-Elysées, we were seated at a table with the owner. The owner was quick to point out to me that his establishment had become very pro-American, and one needed only to look at the showgirls to prove his point. During the Nazi occupation, all his showgirls had sported big breasts (more to the German liking), but now that the Americans had arrived, the show-girls all had smaller breasts (more to the French and American liking). It was one of the most unique demonstrations of Allied support I would ever encounter! The owner was shortly thereafter taken into custody for being a collaborator.

The official liberation of Paris began on 23 August 1944, even though there were German stragglers left behind at isolated points. Brigadier General Jacques-Philippe LeClerc marched down the Champs-Elysées with the French Second Armored Division, and the French people went completely wild at this sight. It must be mentioned, however, that while General LeClerc had to withdraw his division from the front line of combat, the troops were to have gathered after a very short leave and return to their units. It was, however, very difficult for the whole division to assemble in the required time, as the soldiers were taking their leave and reported rather late for their assignments, causing some difficulty in the overall command structure. General Charles de Gaulle unofficially entered Paris on the evening of 25 August, taking up residence in the Hotel de Ville. He made his official entry into the city on 26 August 1944.

Within days, there were many notable Parisians returning to their city from various parts of the world. How they came through the lines remains a mystery to me. However, together with their arrival, came distractions that were not needed at this point in the war effort. For example, Baron Henri de Rothschild insisted upon having a party for the general staff officers at his home in Paris. At this party he served us the greatest wines from his vineyards and a very lavish dinner—a second mystery as to where the food came from. General de Gaulle himself proved a slight hindrance to the ongoing Allied efforts: as the new leader of France he held a reception at Versailles for the Allied general staff. But these distractions stopped immediately, as we could no longer accept such diversions for the task ahead.

We Allies knew that the Germans had left behind agents, and thus we sought out Gestapo headquarters and located the German interrogation center in the Bois de Boulogne. In the basement of the building, the walls were of solid concrete from which protruded chains with arm locks, and between the chains, huge rows of dug-out concrete gave stark evidence that the shackled victims had been tortured and carved their story with their fingernails so posterity could read the madness of this war. There were other instruments of torture, including empty cages that once held humans who, by now, must have been more animal than human.

Some days later in the company of a fellow intelligence officer, I revisited the dwelling, only to learn that now it was taken over by the French, and I saw Nazi collaborators being brought in. The fear on their faces gave evidence that the cycle of madness was being repeated.

Colonel Allen Calvert, chief of ETOUSA's Counter Intelligence Corps, informed me that he had received reports indicating the Germans were collaborating with contacts in the Paris brothels, since they knew Allied soldiers would be visiting these places of recreation soon after their arrival. I embarked upon a few tours of these establishments with Colonel Calvert, and I must admit they were beautifully decorated, not to mention well supplied with attractive girls of every shape, size, and ethnic background. We eventually surmised that the reports Calvert had received possessed little merit but, as a precaution, we advised the French to close down all brothels in the city until the end of hostilities. It was not a popular move, but one that we deemed necessary to the preservation of Allied security. It was to have lasting repercussions, for I subsequently learned that after the war a member of the French Deputies—a woman named Marthe Richard—in 1946 succeeded in having the temporary law made a permanent part of the French legal code. Brothels remain illegal in Paris to this very day.

The French women who had been overly friendly with the Germans felt the wrath of their fellow citizens after the liberation. For many that meant shaved heads and a march through Paris during which the citizens took out their vengeance by spitting on them and other acts of depravity. Later, when I visited Holland, I found the Dutch people duplicating the exact scene with collaborating Dutch women.

Years later, I received a copy of an autobiography written by the Duke of Rohan, a French Resistance officer, with whom I maintained some acquaintance. In the book, I am mentioned for two specific actions: one, I readily admit to—that of closing the houses of prostitution in Paris; the second relates to my decision to allow the French Resistance to take a quantity of cloth to make uniforms for Resistance fighters. While I have only a slight memory of this action, I do know why it was so necessary. The French Resistance fighters needed identification to prevent them from being taken as guerrilla fighters for the Germans. On 19 October 1944, 170 rolls of blue material were shipped from the depot at Vincennes to Rochefort in Terre for the uniforms, which were soon gladly worn by the FFI. The material provided uniforms for over 4,000 men.

It had long been planned that Paris, once secure, would become the center for the troops to have the rest and relaxation (R&R) from the stress of battle. The Paris concept, still a source of argument, was aborted, and many blame Major General J. C. H. Lee, the deputy of ETOUSA for supply and the commander of the Communications Zone (COM Z), for the change. As soon as Paris was secure, General Lee moved a small cadre of his headquarters to Paris and occupied several of the buildings, much to General Eisenhower's displeasure. In defense of General Lee (who in many ways was known as a strict disciplinarian), it was a logical move. Paris was the communications hub for that area of Europe, with telegraph and telephone lines as well as rail lines, and General Lee, in his role of ensuring that supplies arrived for the troops, needed both of these capabilities. In addition, since he was serving under General Eisenhower, all Eisenhower had to do was tell him to move his headquarters, and it would have been done. Though Eisenhower disliked the move, he understood its logic. It should also be noted that General Lee must have done something right, as about this time, General Marshall promoted him to lieutenant general by direct War Department order.

The Communications Zone headquarters decided, instead, to establish the hotel and resort areas available on the Mediterranean, principally those in Cannes, as the R&R center for the American troops. Soon after the 509th Paratrooper Battalion had liberated Cannes on 23 August 1944, I traveled there to assess an unusual situation: intelligence reports had been made pertaining to the fact that enemy activity (on a small scale) was still being conducted in the area. The Germans and the French had been engaged in combat in that area, and I was directed to evaluate the nature of this activity

LE FRONT DE LA VILAINE

et

LA TENTATIVE DU DUC ALAIN DE ROHAN POUR LIBÉRER ST-NAZAIRE EN OCT. 1944

★

Rapports de Le Diagon, P. Le Gal et J.R. Kauffmann

★

★ ★

1913 . 1966

Le Cne Alain duc de Rohan en 1944

★★★

The front of the Villian
and
the Attempt of the Duke
Alain De Rohan to liberate St. Nazaire in Oct 1944

Cover of the Duke of Rohan's autobiography, which includes information on Colonel Hauenstein.

Colonel Hauenstein's reference in the Duke of Rohan's autobiography. Translation from the French: "Colonel R. W. Hauenstein 'Chief Intelligence Branch European Theater' permitted Lt. Guazava to take for our soldiers more than 15 million francs of cloth. It is he, who at the liberation of Paris, closed all the houses of tolerance (prostitution) to keep the Germans from hiding there. This measure exploited for political ends had to be perpetuated for the good of public health."

before troops were sent there. Upon arrival, I learned that the French and Germans were, in fact, conducting a sort of war game, in which a certain number of shells were fired each day, first by the French and then by the Germans. It was not an activity of much military significance, and shortly American forces were sent in to clear out the area.

When I arrived in Cannes, I took a temporary billet at the Carlton Hotel, only to find the staff waiting to serve its new masters, much as the Hotel George V employees had done so many days earlier. I was the first American officer they had met, so I was treated royally. I told them I needed a room for the night, and they immediately assigned me to a suite—the same suite that the Duke and Duchess of Windsor had stayed in during their honeymoon. The management of the hotel asked me if I would be dining there that evening, and I replied that I would. So, after freshening up, I went down for dinner, and indeed they were prepared! When I walked into the dining room, the orchestra immediately starting playing, and waiters attended me hand and foot. This was because, save for my driver and another officer, I was the only patron for dinner that night. Imagine being in a huge European dining room, music playing, waiters everywhere, and you being the only customer. That meal was rather intimidating, and the very next day I moved my lodgings to more austere surroundings, but I will never forget that dinner in Cannes.

Because France was now a full-fledged independent member of the Allied forces again, its military officers soon demanded to be included for consultation on almost every issue, particularly those relating to intelligence. They wished to receive all of the information available to the ETOUSA and SHAEF intelligence staffs. However, this was a demand we were not willing to accommodate, for we didn't know how strongly Allied allegiance would have been allowed to cement in the French psyche after so many months of Nazi occupation. Intelligence derived from ULTRA was not generally passed along to the French or, if it were, it would be sanitized in such a manner that no one would be able to surmise the source of the intelligence.

That the French continued to maintain suspicious attitudes toward the Allied forces was evident in the reaction afforded by one of my directives shortly after liberation. I had realized that we maintained little knowledge of the French infrastructure—railroads, highways, water supplies, communications capabilities, general economics, and so on—all of which is essential knowledge in any area of potential conflict. With this in mind, I sent a directive to all of the base section G-2s in the area, tasking them with the collection and analysis of data related to these aforementioned categories. It was not an unusual task, but one of the G-2s in the Marseilles headquarters left the directive on his desk, where it was seen by a French liaison officer. This officer reported the matter to his French superior. SHAEF headquarters soon received a phone call from General de Gaulle, demanding to know why the Allies were spying on one of their own. It was a source of some controversy, but we prevailed and were able to convince the French of the necessity for such a measure, and they, in fact conducted much of the research for us.

My experiences in Paris as one of the first American officers to soak in the sights of exuberant Allied occupation remain vivid memories to this day. I apparently must have found some favor from the French, for on 27 June 1945 they awarded me the Croix de Guerre with palm—a notable award, indeed—and issued me a citation that read, "For exceptional services of war rendered during the course of the operation for the liberation of France." The citation was signed by none other than Charles de Gaulle, himself.

The memories of Paris have lasted my entire lifetime. One final example is the Puccini opera *La Boheme*. Every time I see the opera or hear an aria from it, I am taken back to the very cold winter of 1944 in Paris. We were invited to a performance of *La Boheme* at the Paris Opera House. The evening came, and it was bitter cold outside (and without heat inside), which made what was happening on the stage that much more poignant. Here were the opera singers on a stage performing an opera set in a very cold apartment in Paris while we, in the audience, sat there shivering in a very cold and elegant opera house. The connection between the singers and the audience was extraordinary.

Though my headquarters remained in Paris, I spent considerable time traveling throughout the war zones in the British, French, and American areas.

NOTE

1. In his book titled *"Coke goes to War,"* V. Dennis Wrynn states that "nearly 200 Coca-Cola company employees were given quasi-military status as TAs (Technical Advisors) and followed the troops to every continent barring Antarctica, providing Coca-Cola to the boys and girls in the service. These TAs wore Army uniforms and were given officer's rank. Two were killed during the war. Most were involved in building or converting existing bottling plants in far-off places with enemy prisoners of war often used as willing workers."

The Campaign Continues in Europe

As the Allied armies advanced across Europe, and particularly as they advanced into areas beyond France, the mission of ETOUSA G-2 became more complicated. Now, in lieu of the French underground, we were more dependent on the Belgian and the Dutch underground efforts. Both of these organizations contributed significantly to the Allied cause.

Additionally, as the American forces began to enter German territory, the role of our base sectors changed considerably. Base sectors were no longer dealing with basically friendly citizens; they were now dealing with German nationals—our enemies—and this change gave rise to a new set of intelligence problems. First, there was a marked difference in the level of cooperation between the U.S. forces and the local citizens; second, there were reports of several possible guerrilla groups that we had to evaluate. These groups consisted of the following:

- "Werewolves": Reportedly the SS and the Hitler Youths were actively recruiting young men and women to operate in a guerrilla mode after the cessation of hostilities. These Werewolves would remain in the occupied areas and continue to cause trouble for the U.S. occupying forces. While sporadic guerrilla activity did occur, we never had concrete proof of such an organization, but it was one of our continuing intelligence concerns.

- The Brandenberg Division: A special force unit was started by Admiral Wilhelm C. Canaris, chief of German intelligence. This group was active throughout the war and operated frequently behind enemy lines, wearing the uniforms of the

125

opposing army and speaking the local language (as reputed during the Battle of the Bulge). The unit was disbanded in 1944 when Admiral Canaris was arrested, and we saw no actual indications of guerrilla operations.

- Otto Skorzeny: He was a figure well known to U.S. intelligence throughout the war years. He often operated under direct orders from Hitler in his special operations. Captured by the Allies in May of 1944, there was no evidence of guerrilla activities on the part of his troops. But we did keep an eye out for such activity.

Another area that took on new significance as we entered Germany was the German nuclear program. Major Tony Calvert and the ALSOS teams became very active as they followed our troops through Germany. Colonel Boris Pash, head of ALSOS, in my opinion, was a loose cannon who needed close watching. I had the responsibility of signing off on his reports and maintaining an awareness of what his teams were doing. Colonel Pash's main asset was his special pass, signed by General Eisenhower. This pass allowed him to move freely throughout Germany to search for men and materials associated with the German nuclear program. His technical assistant was a man named Dr. Samuel A. Goudsmit, a Dutch scientist who had been teaching at an American university and who had a detailed knowledge of nuclear physics.

An example of the German work was discovered with the seizing of data regarding nuclear experiments at Hechingen, the center of German research and development. Intelligence derived from the ALSOS source was not shared with any of the Allied intelligence services, but was sent directly back to Washington.

At the same time, General Leslie M. Groves established a joint U.S./U.K. group under Lt. Colonel John Lansdale Jr., which was responsible for capturing most of the uranium known to be in German control. It was through the work of this group that the Allies knew in April of 1945 that the Germans could not develop the atomic bomb in time to assist them in their war efforts.

Major Paul Neff, served in an effort similar to that of the ALSOS team. He had been assigned as a member of the U.S. Signal Corps team of cryptanalysts assigned to Bletchley Park, to assist with the U.K. code breaking operations. In the spring of 1945, he took on a different mission. He entered Germany with the troops with a specific mission. He was tasked to find members of the German cryptanalytic effort. While I was aware of this activity I did not see the information obtained from these specific prisoners once interrogated.

For both of these groups, Major Calvert was a necessary link. He became the man responsible for moving any equipment, uranium, or personnel associated with the German nuclear program to a port for shipment to the United States. The routes along the way were clearly marked "Calvert's Route" to avoid any confusion; this was good for the drivers, but the ordinary GI got a different impression. There was, at that time, a brand of whiskey made in Baltimore named Calvert, so the GIs kept wondering what was happening to all that good whiskey being transported along the so-called Calvert Route.

I believe that the work of Pash's group, while unorthodox, did, in fact, produce good results. Through his work, most of the German scientific personnel were under American control, thereby preventing the Russians from exploiting their knowledge, and the majority of their equipment and documentation remained in American hands. This is surely not a small contribution from a rather unique group of individuals.

As the Allied armies continued their advance across the European continent, they apprehended a number of Russian prisoners of war, some of them German collaborators and others slave laborers who had been captured and put to work by the Germans. These Russians were particularly happy to be in American hands and, despite the fact that their home country had been one of our Allies, did not wish to return to the Communist regime that existed therein.

We consequently found them to be an excellent intelligence source—particularly regarding German morale and the state of that nation's industrial efforts. We began interrogating the Russians in American custody; they were ready to talk (many in hopes of staying in American hands). Their input was of high value to the war effort, and it got a lot of attention until one of the recipients, in Washington, chanced to ask, "Where does this intelligence come from?" When it was revealed that we were interrogating Russians, we soon received orders from the War Department to shut down the operation, since Russia was our ally and thus its prisoners should not be subject to Allied interrogation. We did not, however, pass on this directive, but kept it going informally. Good sources of intelligence information were needed.

General Eisenhower at this point ordered that these Russian prisoners and slave laborers were to be sent back to their mother country even though many of them feared that prospect and even though the Russians failed to allow Allied observers behind Polish lines to look for American prisoners.

What we didn't know was that, as early as April of 1944 (months before the D-day invasion) the question of what to do about Russians serving in the German army when captured by the Allies had arisen at the highest levels of the American government. Secretary of War Stimpson wanted the Russians treated under the Geneva Convention, allowing those who did not want to be repatriated to remain in Allied hands. As late as January of 1945 this was the prevailing view from both the secretary of war and the U.S. attorney general. Apparently their view was reversed at a higher level, namely that of the president of the United States. General Marshall had informed General Eisenhower that "our bosses believe that we've just got to keep Russia in the war and therefore we've got to handle them with kid gloves—or they'll do a France on us. So treat with them. Do your best to get along with them."

Based on Marshall's orders, the Russian prisoners of war and the slave laborers were sent back to Russia, even though many feared they faced death upon return. The order was based on political reasoning. Eisenhower is quoted as saying, "I mean, we were supposed to send them back by force. We didn't even think about it. I forget how many suicides we had one night."

In contrast, the Russians were refusing to allow American observers behind the Russian lines in Poland to look for American POWs. The author of *Marching Orders*, Bruce Lee, reports the following:

Located one such American prisoner, who was captured in Africa and liberated by the Russians in Poland. He was offered the choice of being shot along with the other Russian prisoners in the camp, or fighting his way into Berlin with the Red Army. He chose Berlin, shooting his way through the city. When the fighting stopped, he was congratulated for his competence in killing Germans by his Russian battalion Commander, given a special pass, a small sack of potatoes and was told to walk west to the Elbe where the Americans were encamped.

Thus the final decision apparently had as much to do with the return of the liberated Americans from German POW camps as it did with the diplomatic front. The final quid pro quo for the Americans was that if you (Russia) return our liberated ex-German-held prisoners of war to the Allies, we, the Allies, will return the Russian prisoners of war who fought for the Germans to Russia.

Nowhere was the assertion more evident than in what appeared to be a failure of U.S. intelligence to project, in late 1944, that the Germans were planning a counteroffensive measure. This offensive came to be called the Battle of the Bulge. Nazi officers had been establishing armies on the western front, equipping them with tanks and positioning them in such a manner as to play on Allied weaknesses in the Ardennes. They then planned to advance into Antwerp (a main port for incoming Allied supplies) and to separate American soldiers in the south from British forces in the north. The Germans had been careful to prepare for the offensive with the utmost secrecy, since they knew America would not be expecting a counterassault. Indeed, we had received no clear indications that the Nazis were massing for attack; all the communications were within Germany and on landline, so ULTRA provided no warnings, and neither did photo reconnaissance or any other intelligence source. From 16 December 1944 to 16 January 1945 German and Allied forces clashed, and, although the outcome was an eventual Allied victory, the lessons learned from this assault forces us to seriously re-examine our intelligence operations.

Surprisingly, the lapses were not as serious as had been expected. Before the attack, Colonel (Tick) Bonesteel, son of Major General Bonesteel, member of a special intelligence unit and a good friend of mine, had asked me whether we had any indications that German units were massing for a surprise attack on our front. He believed that activity in this region had died down to a pronounced degree, becoming too quiet, and that analysis of the German order of battle indicated that certain units could not be accounted for. I conferred with General Bryan Conrad, my G-2, who proposed that I fly to Washington under the guise that I was taking a well-deserved leave, but I actually visited headquarters to obtain counsel regarding the possibility of a German counterattack. At the War Department, I requested a briefing with a European expert, a Harvard professor named Dr. Donald McKay, and with other officials, but the briefing fell on deaf ears. Verification was never given to prepare for such an assault. Somewhat frustrated, I traveled home to spend Christmas with my family in Grand Rapids, for there was nothing else I could do. The Battle of the Bulge soon commenced, exactly as it had been predicted by Colonel Bonesteel and by other individuals, including Colonel Oscar Koch, the G-2 of General Patton's army, and I was ordered back to Europe. Thus, it can be asserted that American intelligence received indications that such an assault would happen but that its command had simply failed to recognize them. One of the perceived problems is that, by this time of the war, the ULTRA (ENIGMA) information was being received with such timely consistency, and it contained such valuable information, that senior officials fell into the trap of believing if any information was not in ULTRA, that reported event was not going to happen. It also revealed the intelligence gap of ULTRA officers who lacked understanding of the full importance of order of battle.

And although we knew of the special force units employed by the Nazis—whereby German soldiers dressed in American Army uniforms and speaking perfect English infiltrated into our line—we had no advance information of such an occurrence during the Battle of the Bulge. These specific troops were closely watched by the CIC elements of SHAEF and ETOUSA. Over time we had heard many rumors of such a unit attempting to assassinate General Eisenhower and, in fact, had found a U.S. Army lieutenant colonel who resembled Eisenhower, and he became a frequent impersonator of the general in public.

While we had no clear indications from ULTRA of the Germans massing for an attack, there was a red flag in the MAGIC traffic[1] from Baron Oshima. On 14 November 1944 he reported back to Tokyo that Hitler was planning a major counteroffensive in the West, with time and place as yet undisclosed. Baron Oshima cast doubt on the German capability to conduct such a counteroffensive, thereby weakening the Allies' acceptance of his reporting.

U.S. intelligence is also faulted for its lack of expediency in recognizing the existence of the Holocaust. At no time during the war did ETOUSA G-2 receive any intelligence regarding the holocaust activities in Europe. The British had gained some indications of these atrocities through their interception of ULTRA messages, but these reports were carefully censored before they were passed on to us. Thus when I accompanied the troops that liberated the Dachau concentration camp outside of Munich, I found myself appalled that such an

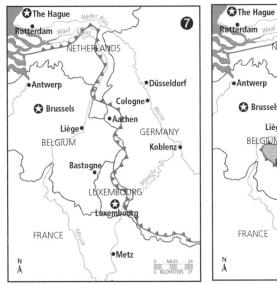

Map of Europe with inset of location of the Battle of the Bulge (TOP). *Allied line as of 16 December 1944* (BOTTOM LEFT), *prior to the Battle of the Bulge. The German troops, located inside Germany, did not have to depend on ENIGMA/radio for communications; they could employ landline communications or couriers. The German line as of 22 December 1944* (BOTTOM RIGHT), *during its penetration in the Battle of the Bulge. At this point, the German army was outside of the German homeland and was dependent once again on ENIGMA/radio for communications.*

entity could have existed beneath our American intelligence radar. As we stepped through the front gates, we found the Nazis still putting bodies into the ovens. We also came upon several boxcars waiting to be unloaded, filled with the bodies of the living and the dead. The living had survived only by eating the vital organs of their deceased fellow prisoners. What a ghastly sight!

A prisoner approached us and told us to go to the nearby water tank and see if anyone was, in fact, in the tank. When we arrived at the tank, we found a nude male prisoner submerged in the tank. The Germans were conducting a human experiment with the prisoner. At the request of the German air force they were testing to see how long a human could survive in water and at what temperature. The poor emaciated prisoner was taken out of the tank and given a blanket to cover his nude body. He appeared to be so stunned with his rescue that he could barely talk. I will never forget this poor unfortunate man. I had a picture taken as evidence of the German maltreatment of prisoners.

As I continued to walk through the camp, I came upon another gruesome scene. It was a wall with wrist shackles mounted high on the wall. When I asked the purpose, I was told that male prisoners were suspended from the shackles on the wall. Cord was then tied around their testicles with a stick on the end. The Germans had trained dogs to then jump up and pull the stick, thereby inflicting great pain on the suspended prisoners. About this time, one of the vicious dogs appeared, and, without any hesitation, we shot him. My sergeant took a picture of the dead dog. Such terrible torture!

I then interrogated the camp commandant, who had on his desk three lamps with shades made from the skins of inmates, and I found him to be cold, aloof, and of no value from an intelligence point of view. His icy demeanor prompted one of my men to draw a pistol as though to dispatch him, but we restrained him. I had never before seen anything akin to what I saw in that concentration camp, and I certainly hoped the world would never see such atrocities again.

As I left the camp, I had my aide take one final photograph of the sights we had seen. It depicts the German guards collected in one area within barbed wire, with the prisoners they so brutally treated looking on. In some extreme cases, the liberating forces had been so affected by what they saw that the German guards were summarily shot on sight.

Dachau prisoner rescued from water tank, 1945. Colonel Hauenstein is on the right.

Dog killed in concentration camp by Colonel Hauenstein, 1945.

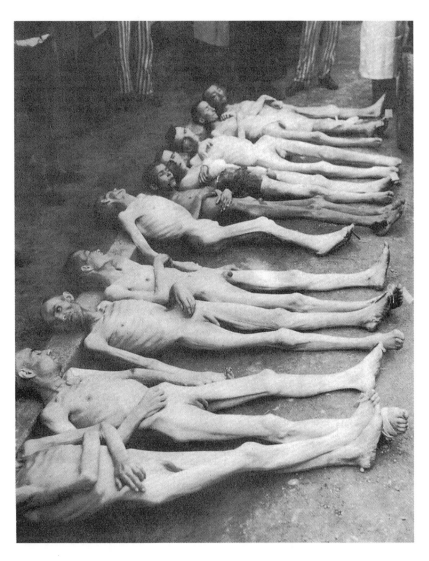

Corpses of male prisoners, Dachau prison camp, 1945.

Captured German guards, Dachau, 1945.

As a side note: during the liberation of Dachau, my men happened to take pictures of the ovens used to cremate prisoners and noticed the brand name of a German manufacturer embossed on the doors. The name became permanently etched into my brain. Years later, as an international buyer of food machinery, I was up for a contract with a large bakery in New York that produced Kosher baked goods. I found out that my sole competition was the German manufacturing firm who had produced the ovens at Dachau. I dug up the photo, showed it to representatives from the bakery, and soon thereafter was awarded the contract. It was to this camp that General Eisenhower took the entire citizenry of the local town to view the horrors.[2]

Toward the end of the war, as Allied victory became ever more certain, General Eisenhower transferred the army of Field Marshall Bernard Montgomery, a commander of British troops, to northern Germany (the Lubeck area). This move was not done in reprisal for Montgomery's opposition to the method with which the Allies should have attempted a capture of Berlin, as many historians have surmised. Montgomery had wished to deploy his troops to the German capital as soon as possible and to capture it before the Russian Red Army could get there. General Eisenhower disagreed because he knew the recent Yalta Conference had split postwar Germany into four sections and Berlin would be in the center of the Russian Zone. He did, however, transfer Montgomery because of a Communist threat, not to Berlin but to Scandinavia. The Japanese ambassador in Moscow had reported back to Tokyo that Stalin was planning to break his agreement with the Allies to keep his troops out of Denmark. General Eisenhower consequently believed that Allied forces were needed in northern Germany to monitor Russian activity in that region.

About this time, two heads of the intelligence division of the Dutch Army approached me about the possibility of having some of their officers collaborate with ETOUSA intelligence. The Netherlands had been one of the first nations overrun by Nazi forces, and now the newly freed country wished to learn intelligence operations and send officers to units of our command. The Dutch had initially approached ETOUSA headquarters about this possibility. Since headquarters did not want to deal with the matter, it was referred to me. It was quite impossible to honor their request due to classified requirements, despite the fact that the Dutch offered me their highest decoration if I would agree with their proposed collaboration.

NOTES

1. The MAGIC message of 14 November 1944 was decrypted and distributed to U.S. authorities on 23 November 1944.
2. The majority of the early reportings of the executions were encoded using the German police code and not the ENIGMA. The system became virtually unreadable after February 1943. The SS ENIGMA traffic ceased on the radio nets in February 1943 and only sparsely reappeared in the spring of 1945. There was sporadic reporting of executions in the Japanese MAGIC diplomatic traffic sent from ambassadors in Russia and Germany.

Final Days

January 1945 to May 1945

As the Allied forces pushed farther into Germany, our intelligence efforts continued, and for ETOUSA, one of our main focus points was a continued effort in the area of technical intelligence. We worked hard to ensure that the advancing troops were advised of specific areas of interest to the U.S. for technical intelligence, whether it be a town, a plant, or even personnel. That effort continued right up to the time of the German surrender.

One specific area of interest in the technical area was the German attempts at developing advanced aircraft. We knew early in the war that the Germans were experimenting with jet propulsion as early as 1942. On 25 July 1944, an ME-262 became the world's first operational jet fighter. Our pilots returning from their missions soon began reporting the presence of new enemies in the sky. Photo reconnaissance revealed these enemies to be high-speed aircraft making use of jet engine technology. We identified the craft as P16s because of their wingspans (we thought 16 feet across), later identified by the Germans as the ME-262 (Schwalbe or Swallow), and, through the use of secret agents and aerial photography, we kept an eye on their continued development. Fortunately for the Allies, although 1,443 of the ME-262 aircraft were produced, only about 300 of them saw combat. The Germans were short of fuel, as well as qualified pilots. Late in the war, the USAAF (United States Army Air Force) established Operation LUSTY under Colonel Harold M. Watson, with a mission to locate and capture as many of the advanced German aircraft as possible.

After the Allies made their first inroads into Germany, I knew Allied victory had been secured and that the long road to war was about to end. One day I was in a jeep going through a small German village when I saw a column of German prisoners of war approaching. What appalled me was the fact that the German residents of the village all rushed out of their homes and cheered the Germans as they marched along. I had a very strong urge to break up this adulation— but I did not. The strong sentiment against the German military by the U.S. military forces took many forms, some of which resulted in a slight twist of humor. Once, when I visited with Lt. Colonel Donald Thackery, the G-2 of the Fifth Division in Germany, such an occasion arose. Colonel Thackery had taken an Iron Cross medal from a German prisoner of war and placed it around the neck of an adopted dog. The dog wore the medal with a great deal of pride. There may have been a war going on, but the dog had no problem at all in changing sides.

U.S. intelligence received a hefty shock in March of 1945. It seems that on 11 March the Russian military authorities sent a message via the American Mission in Moscow to the War Department in Washington—not to the Allied Command in Europe. The message contained a request for the Americans to bomb a location 5½ kilometers southeast of Zossen and 1 to 1½ miles east of the autobahn running from Berlin to Dresden. The reason for the bombing request was that, apparently in 1939, the German army had built an underground "citadel." The structure covered about six acres underground and was the German army's equivalent of the U.S. Pentagon. We had no idea of the existence of this structure until advised of its existence by the Russians, and in researching our information, we could not uncover any intelligence in our files regarding this "citadel." The bombing raid was conducted on 15 March 1945 but resulted in only superficial damage. The structure was later used by the Russians for the group of Soviet forces in Germany.

Late in the war, I was with the Army Group in the Garmisch-Partenkirchen area in southern Germany. Our forces were there to prevent Hitler and his henchmen from fleeing to his Eagle's Nest. There was a constant argument between the Joint Intelligence Committee members who said "Yes" to a Nazi redoubt, and OSS who constantly said "No." The OSS analysis was based on the fact that no captured high-level German officer ever expressed knowledge of such a redoubt when interrogated. I chose to take a look for myself, so using my "power" pass, off I went.

While in the area, I was privy to several incidents of historical import. First, on 1 May 1945 General von Rundstedt, a highly respected commander in the German army, surrendered to our forces

Colonel Thackery and his medaled dog. Lt. Colonel Thackery (CENTER), *Colonel Hauenstein* (LEFT).

Colonel Hauenstein in Czechoslovakia, 30 April 1945. Left to right: Colonel Hauenstein; his adjutant, Major Taylor; and Captain Robinson, armored car driver.

at Bad Tolz in Austria. General von Rundstedt, a true Prussian-trained general, was highly respected by the Allies. He had been tapped to lead the German invasion of England, had fought on the Russian front, and later had been assigned to defend the German defenses facing the invasion. When I arrived, I found the general hardly looking like the epitome of a Prussian officer. He appeared tired and dejected. As I approached, I was told that the first thing Rundstedt's aide and physician said to the captors was that the general required a bottle of cognac ever day for his health! That reminded me of his office in Paris, where I had found all the cognac bottles. During my interrogation of him, I asked why he hadn't chased the British after driving them from the European continent during the Battle of Dunkirk, early in the war. His response was, "Did you ever try to fight a battleship with a rowboat?" (Thus acknowledging Britain's superior naval power.) I also asked von Rundstedt if he knew where Hitler was hiding. He replied, "No, but I imagine he is up in the mountains herding sheep, where he belongs."[1] He was not a fan of Hitler, but a Prussian general who followed orders.

Second, at about the same time, 9 May 1945, Reichsmarschal Hermann Goering, head of the German air force, surrendered to troops of the 42nd Infantry Division in the Tyrol area of Austria. I was not present but heard that he had been captured carrying a field marshal's baton. I was told that he refused to give it up, declaring it was a symbol of his rank. The story was that when it was finally taken from him, it rattled, and when it was opened it was found to be full of precious gems—perhaps to buy his freedom. I did not see the baton at the time,[2] but I heard that it was given to President Harry S. Truman in a ceremony at the White House.

Later, I learned that two of Hermann Goering's batons were in American museums. One, ivory in color, with a solid core, is at West Point—it had been presented to Truman by General Patch, commander of the Seventh Army, on the lawn of the White House on 5 July 1945. A second, darker in color and hollow on the inside, with a removable end, is at Fort Benning in Georgia. It was reportedly found at Berchtsgaten on 7 May 1945 with Goering's other hidden treasures. If it was the one involved in the story relayed to me, perhaps the value of its onetime contents explains its absence from Army inventory—it disappeared and was not recovered until 1948. We will never know, but I am resolute in my memory of what was relayed to me about the baton in May of 1945.

Reichsmarschal Hermann Goering's captured baton with the hollow core.

Finally, during this same time period, Hungarian refugees arrived at Mattsee, in the American zone of Austria, carrying a large chest that was given to the U.S. Army for safekeeping. By pure happenstance I was with the unit that received the chest. The chest was turned over in my presence, and, as the senior U.S. Army officer present, I had it opened. To our amazement, we discovered the chest was full of jewels, some loose and some set into objects. The Hungarians were particularly concerned about the safety of one item in the chest. It was a very old gem-encrusted crown, obviously an important relic of Hungarian history. To our shock and utter amazement, we learned it was the crown of St. Stephen.[3] It was being given to the U.S. forces to protect it from falling into Soviet hands. The chest and jewels were transported to Seventh Army headquarters, and a Hungarian guard accompanied the treasures until they were safely secured.

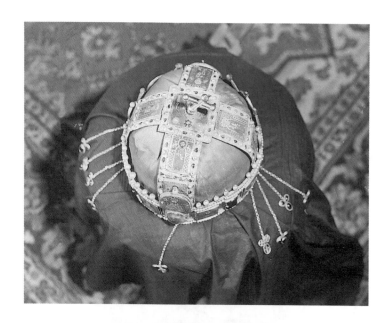

The crown and orb of St. Stephen, first king of Hungary. The Hungarian crown jewels were given to U.S. forces and then placed into the U.S. Army repository in Frankfurt, Germany. These photos were taken by the Signal Corps at the time of the initial turnover of the jewels to U.S. forces.

Colonel Hauenstein and Hungarians meet at Mattsee, Austria. Colonel Hauenstein was enroute to the Bavarian area of Germany to look into the reports of German officials escaping to the Eagle's Nest. The Hungarians were fleeing from the Russian army and wanted to get the Hungarian crown jewels into American hands. The two routes crossed at Mattsee.

During my time in southern Germany and Austria, I was absolutely amazed at the number of German troops who were fleeing ahead of the Russian occupation of Austria. They were coming in hordes to be captured by the Americans instead of the Russians. A great many were Nazi Storm Troopers (SS), by all appearances a very nasty group of individuals. But they were very happy to have made it to the arms of the American captors. It was difficult for Americans to treat them with an even hand, especially since we all knew of the Storm Trooper's treatment of natives in their occupied lands.

NOTES

1. General von Rundstedt was the former commander-in-chief for the defense of the European coast and the French Mediterranean coastal areas. He was not tried as a war criminal but held by the British under house arrest for possible trial for four years. He died on 1 February 1953.

2. Hermann Goering was tried as a war criminal at Nuremberg, Germany, for crimes against humanity and war crimes. He was found guilty of all charges and sentenced to be hanged on 15 October 1946. Just two hours before his execution, he committed suicide by taking potassium cyanide poison.

3. The Nazi Prime Minister of Hungary, Jeno Szollosi, along with a group of Hungarian refugees, fled Hungary with a Gestapo guard prior to the Russian invasions of Hungary. Among the treasures they took with them was the crown of St. Stephen. The Gestapo took the group to Mattsee, Austria, where they deserted the group. The Anti-Tank Company, 342nd Infantry, captured them along with the chest. The crown remained in American hands until it was returned to Hungary by President Jimmy Carter. Prime Minister Szollozi was returned to Hungary and executed as a war criminal.

Postsurrender

May 1945 to July 1945

For me, one of the pinnacle events of my life is the day that Germany surrendered to the Allied forces—it was one of both satisfaction and jubilation! However, with the German surrender, we almost immediately were faced with the problem of transferring troops to the Pacific Theater. One of our main concerns was the possibility of real discontent among the troops selected to be transferred; having "won" their part of the war, would they object to entering another? We were all very proud of the troops, who had no real problem with this issue; this was war, and let's get it over in a hurry. The training of our troops was so complete that they understood and accepted.

Almost immediately after the surrender of Germany, as the Allies were joining up with the Russians, I received an unusual request. It had come through channels to provide a certain Captain Peter Schouvaloff of my staff to be assigned as an interpreter and translator for Marshall Georgi Konstantinovich Zhukov, the commander of the Russian Army now occupying a sector of Germany. Captain Schouvaloff was an officer who had joined the American forces and was now an American citizen. His father had been Count Peter H. Schouvaloff and a rather famous Russian. I learned that the elder Schouvaloff had been in command of an army of White Russians, and it seemed that Zhukov had been a private in his army during the revolution. Zhukov had heard that we had his son, Captain Schouvaloff, better known as Count Schouvaloff, now in our service and wanted to meet with him to use him as a translator. Schouvaloff was a rather interesting character. I had previously made him available to General Matthew Ridgeway, while on my staff, who was seeking a French interpreter for D-day landings from aircraft. Since Schouvaloff was also fluent in French, I gave the assignment to him, despite the fact that the poor fellow had never jumped from an airplane and had

absolutely flat feet. He did, however, carry out the mission successfully and was recognized by General Ridgeway, who sent a letter com-
mending him for his services. Schouvaloff, while living in America,
had married the daughter of the famous Russian opera singer
Alexander Shelepin.

When Schouvaloff had been assigned to Zhukov for little more
than a week, he returned to my office with red eyes and looked in terrible condition—obviously from a period of heavy drinking. He
merely saluted and remarked, "Some people have given their lives for
their country; I have just given my liver." With that he gave another
salute and walked out. I did not see him again for a week or so. When
he returned, sober and ready for duty, he carried on as an excellent
officer once more. After the war, I had opportunities to see Schouvaloff again in Paris, where he had been assigned by our government
in some special intelligence activities. He obviously was true to form,
as not too many years later, he died of cancer of the liver.

In the summer of 1945, Lt. Colonel Henry C. Claussen came to
Europe to question various personnel, currently serving in Europe,
who were either in the War Department or Hawaii just prior to the
attack on Pearl Harbor. His investigation was extremely sensitive, and
very little of it was discussed with members of my staff. We basically
served as his storage facility and facilitators for the investigation.
Colonel Claussen used ETOUSA rather than the Allied Command, as
his investigation was strictly an American issue and he did not want
to get the British involved in the investigation. I served as his facili-
tator and contact. The wounds of Pearl Harbor were still fresh in the
U.S. military, and the continuing investigation now included the
European theater.

Shortly after hostilities ended, officers of the general staff of SHAEF
and ETOUSA were ordered to appear at the Arc de Triomphe and
attend a ceremony at which the self-proclaimed president of France,
General de Gaulle, would honor the officers' wartime efforts. In other
words, all of the officers of the two commands, from General Eisenhower down for both the U.S. and the U.K. Commands were to be in
attendance. We formed a circle around the Arc and awaited the arrival
of President de Gaulle. We stood there for an interminable length of
time, awaiting his arrival, and finally we could hear shouts coming
from down the Champs-Elysées. There came the president, standing
in his car waving to the people along the street, as he approached the
Arc de Triomphe. When he arrived, rather than stopping immediately,

WAR DEPARTMENT.
Washington, 1 August 1945.

Memorandum for Mr. Bundy.
Subject: Fourth Progress Report of Colonel Clausen's Investigation Supplementary to Army Pearl Harbor Board.

    I. Activities Reported: Investigations at Blandford, Blenchley Park, London, England; Cannes, Marseille, Paris, Versailles, France; Casserta, Italy; Berlin, Frankfurt on Main, Potsdam, Germany; and Washington D.C., were conducted during 15 May to 1 August 1945.

      a. Army Personnel Interviewed:
        Lt. General Leonard T. Gerow
        Lt. General W. B. Smith
        Maj. General John R. Deane
        Brig. General Thomas J. Betts
        Colonel George W. Bicknell
        Colonel Rufus S. Bratton
        Colonel Warren J. Clear
        Colonel Robert E. Schukraft
        Major Louis Stone
      b. British Navy Personnel Interviewed:
        Captain Edward Hastings
      c. Civilians Interviewed:
        Dr. Stanley Hombeck
        George W. Renchard
        John F. Stone
      d. Related Conferences:
        Harvey H. Bundy
        General Thomas T. Handy
        Maj. General Myron C. Cramer
        Maj. General Otto Nelson
        Brig. General Carter Clarke
[250]   Brig. General Thomas North
        Brig. General G. Bryan Conrad
        Brig. General Marion Van Voorst
        Colonel C. W. Christenberry
        Colonel R. W. Hauenstein
        Colonel F. W. Hilles
        Captain Wm. T. Carnahan
        Captain Edmund H. Kellogg
        John F. Sonnett
        Admiral Henry K. Hewitt
      e. Affidavit Evidence Obtained:
        Lt. General Leonard T. Gerow
        Lt. General W. B. Smith
        Maj. General John R. Deane
        Colonel George W. Bicknell
        Colonel Rufus S. Bratton
        Colonel Robert E. Schukraft
        George W. Renchard
        John F. Stone
        Brig Gen. Thomas J. Betts

Points of contact for Colonel Henry C. Claussen's investigation into the Pearl Harbor attack.

The Croix de Guerre presented to Colonel Hauenstein on 27 June 1945.

and recognizing the senior officers present, he made a complete tour around the Arc. He then proceeded to give recognition and decorations to the various officers. It appeared to all of us that it was a complete insult that such an incident would take place. It served to further enforce the negative feelings that many of the officers held regarding de Gaulle. It was at this ceremony that I received my Croix de Guerre, but I decided not to wait in line that long, and consequently it was delivered to me at a later time.

After the end of the war, I had only a short time in postwar Germany, as I was high on the point list for redeployment to the States. Effective 1 July 1945, ETOUSA became United States Forces European Theater (USFET), headquartered in Frankfurt. USFET with a dual role: first, governing the American Sector of Germany; second, serving as the command for the U.S. occupation forces in Germany. General Lucius D. Clay, Eisenhower's deputy was the principal U.S. Army officer handling the governing of the American Sector of Germany. This was an interesting time, as our previous enemy was now a segmented nation that had to be brought back into world society.

General Eisenhower, who was known to have a definite hatred for the German military and what they had inflicted on the world, now was responsible for the German people's reentry into a postwar environment. His attitude of a wary benevolence to the Germans spread throughout his command and greatly assisted in making the task a challenge, though not a repugnant operation. He was of the opinion that civilians should take over the governing functions as soon as the military threat had ceased. This change would involve the German people in the reconstruction of their country.

At the conflict's end, I was involved in the transition of a wartime intelligence operation to a new concept of establishing intelligence priorities for an occupying army in Germany. The transition required not only developing the intelligence for the army but also assisting in establishing the role of the OSS in a peacetime environment. Our main mission for the U.S. Army intelligence personnel in occupied Germany consisted of developing intelligence on the activities of the following:

- Underground military, paramilitary, and political organizations
- Former Nazi leaders, personalities, and organizations
- Counteractivities to the military, political, and economic terms of the surrender
- Counteractivities to the currency-control regulations
- Black market and hoarding
- Locating property stolen from other countries by the Germans
- Locating the assets held in other countries by German nationals or their nominees
- Locating evidence leading to the identification, apprehension, and conviction of war criminals

All of this was a major shift of effort but equally important.

I returned to the United States on 1 July 1945. My role as an intelligence officer during this conflict was but one of millions working together to bring about Allied victory in a conflict of greater magnitude than any before. It had been a long tour of duty, difficult for my family and for myself, but the memories enriched me, made me a stronger person, and imbued in me a deep-seated pride for my country, my countrymen, and my own role in securing their preservation and safety.

My new assignment was to the Pentagon, where I eventually "managed" my own discharge orders. While assigned to the Pentagon, I was tasked to assist with the selection of candidates to man the newly formed Central Intelligence Agency. Since I had worked with most of the intelligence personnel in Europe, I knew which ones would be suitable recruits for the agency. One of the men recruited was William H. Jackson, who later became the deputy director of the agency. Jackson was typical of several highly qualified individuals who were given commissions in the U.S. Army without any form of military instruction. He was initially assigned to the special and highly classified ULTRA Project working through the British at Bletchley Park and later served as an intelligence officer in the 12th Corps. He was a fast learner and became very proficient in the world of intelligence.

When President Truman was at the Potsdam Conference in July 1945, all of us at the Pentagon followed the events closely. I was particularly taken by General Eisenhower's comment stating that he did not know about the atomic bomb until Secretary of War Stimson told him about it on 16 July 1945 at Potsdam. My first thought was that this could not be true, and then I realized what Eisenhower was doing. He was protecting a national secret by being very narrow in his response—he said he knew nothing of the atomic bomb prior to this and did not mention that he knew about the work going on in the MANHATTAN Project. These statements continued to bother me, so I created a timeline as follows:

6 June 1942: The U.S. Army takes over control of the MANHATTAN Project, with General Groves in command. Eisenhower is serving as assistant chief of staff, Operations Division, in Washington, D.C., at the time.

15 June 1942: Eisenhower is assigned to England as the commander, European Theater of Operations, U.S. Army—a new command.

19 August 1943: Roosevelt and Churchill meet at Quebec and agree on timelines for the defeat of Germany and Japan. The war in Europe will be the first priority, followed by Japan. They also develop a timeline for the development of nuclear fission (a signed secret protocol to the Quebec Conference). The timeline for nuclear fission development is beyond the estimated time for the defeat of Germany but not for Japan.

October 1943: "Then almost before I was aware of what had happened, the President had reversed our roles and he was briefing me. America's scientific resources, he said, had been recruited in a staggering project to unlock the secrets of nuclear fission. He believed they could produce a weapon that would totally revolutionize warfare. The President called it an 'atomic bomb.'" (Quoted from *A Soldier's Story* by General Omar N. Bradley.)

5 and 12 January 1944: Eisenhower has private meetings with President Roosevelt, on 5 January from 10:00 to 11:45 and on 12 January from 10:30 to 11:25. No record was kept of the conversation. At his press conference of 18 January 1944 Roosevelt mentions having seen Eisenhower. No further details are available.

January 1944: Major Horace K. Calvert of the MANHATTAN Project staff in Washington is reassigned to London as a member of the American Embassy staff. Major Calvert was dispatched to London, as he told me, "to tell our Theater commander about the Atomic bomb."

April 1944: President Roosevelt sends Danish scientist Niels Bohr to England to discuss nuclear proliferation issues with Churchill. He remains in the U.K. until D-day. He meets with Eisenhower prior to the D-day invasion.

Spring 1944: General Groves of the MANHATTAN Project sends Colonel Arthur V. Peterson to England to brief General Eisenhower on the danger that the Germans might use "radioactive poisons" against the Allied invasion force.

Spring 1944: "From time to time during the spring months staff officers from Washington arrived at my headquarters to give me the latest calculations concerning German progress in the development of new weapons, including as possibilities bacteriological and atomic weapons. *These reports were highly secret and were invariably delivered to me by word of mouth. I was told that the American scientists were making progress in these two types and that as a result of their own experience they were able to make shrewd guesses concerning some of the details of similar German activity. All of this information was supplemented by the periodic reports of intelligence* *agencies in London."* (Quoted from *Crusade in Europe*, by Dwight D. Eisenhower; italics added for emphasis.)

13 June 1944: The Anglo-American Declaration of Trust was signed by the U.S. and the U.K. to, in its own words, "insure the acquisition at the earliest practicable moment of an adequate supply of uranium and thorium 'ores' and to control to the fullest extent practicable the supplies of uranium and thorium ores within the boundaries of such areas as come under their respective jurisdictions."

16 July 1945: "I had a long talk with secretary Stimson, who told me that very shortly there would be a test in New Mexico of the atomic bomb, which American scientists had finally succeeded in developing. The results of the successful test were soon communicated to the Secretary of War by cable. He was tremendously relieved, for he had apparently followed the development with intense interest and felt a keen sense of responsibility for the amount of money and resources that had been devoted to it. I expressed the hope that we would never have to use such a thing against any enemy because I disliked seeing the United States take the lead in introducing into war something as horrible and destructive as this new weapon was described to be." (Quoted from *Crusade in Europe*, by Dwight D. Eisenhower.)

So was Eisenhower telling the truth about the atomic bomb? The answer is, yes and no. He was obviously protecting sensitive information by providing a narrow response. It is truly inconceivable that the man charged with the planning and execution of that plan in the defeat of Germany would not be told during the planning process that research was ongoing to produce an atomic bomb and, most important, that the nuclear capability would not be available for use in Europe, even if desired. Particularly since President Roosevelt had already, in October 1943, informed General Bradley, one of Eisenhower's future subordinates about the potential development of an atomic bomb. And Major Tony Calvert had briefed me on the subject in early 1944.

I was relieved from active duty with the United States Army on 26 June 1946. It had been a long stint of duty, difficult for my family, but a phase of my life that I have always been very proud of, as is my family.

Not long after I returned to civilian life I was informed that I was to be awarded the Order of the British Empire (OBE) for my wartime participation. The medal was presented to me in New York on the British liner the *Mauratania*. The following is an excerpt from the order:

21 August 1945
BHAM (USA)

Dear Vesey:

Many thanks for your letter of 8th August (68/gen/7909) about awards for American recommended by the Head of Agency, C.A.L.A.

The scale of the under mentioned awards is approved and as General Eisenhower has agreed the way seems clear for the War Office to submit the names to the king.

* * *

Colonel Ralph W. Hauenstein

* * *
/s/ R. U. E. Knox

Order of the British Empire (OBE) presented to Colonel Hauenstein, 1946.

I did not cut my ties with the United States Army completely, as I remained in the Ready Reserves for some years. When the Korean War broke out, General Gavin, the famed wartime commander of the 101st Airborne Division, got in touch with me. He wanted me to come back into the Army and serve in his new command as the intelligence officer. I was flattered by the request but declined the offer. My days as a United States military intelligence officer were over—not forgotten then or now, but over. However, I still have an intelligence officer's mind set—when I read the newspaper, I often think, "I wonder what is really going on here?" That attitude will remain with me forever.

Afterthoughts

As in any period of history, the personalities and capabilities of the main players had an impact. I am often asked about how we won the war, and people ask my views on specific individuals whom I observed in action. These opinions are mine alone and are based on my own personal experiences.

How Did We Win?

As to how we won the war, I have a clear answer. We won the battle of logistics, coupled with superb leadership. We had an excellent supply system that was very capable of moving ahead with the troops and meeting their immediate needs. Without such a system, an army is rendered ineffectual. Yes, we had good intelligence as well, but to me the key element of our success was the U.S. logistics system and outstanding leadership.

American Generals

Regarding some of the American generals involved in World War II, my personal observations are as follows:

- Eisenhower was a good military strategist and an excellent diplomat. No other person could have done what he did in amalgamating diverse elements into a cohesive, multinational organization.

- Bradley was a wonderful human being and the best tactical general in the entire war. He was way ahead of Montgomery in strategy.

- Patton speaks for himself.

British Generals

British generals had somewhat the same attitude as British intelligence officials: "You Americans have a lot to learn, so we will teach you—we are experienced."

- Montgomery was a real martinet. He often held the ULTRA information to himself when discussing strategy with his staff. He was not at all a team player.

American Intelligence Officers

- Colonel Monk Dickson was the best combat force G-2 in the American Army. He was good in Africa and should have been the G-2 of the Army Group but was outranked by General Sibert, who was given the choice of remaining the G-2 of ETOUSA or going with Bradley. (I worked under Sibert and felt he was less effective than Dickson and some others.)

- Colonel Koch was highly prized by General Patton, who felt his G-2 was brilliant and made many attempts to have him promoted to brigadier general (to no avail). Patton had good reason for feeling as he did because he held ULTRA in low regard and left all such matters up to Koch. Naturally, with such "insight" Koch appeared an absolute genius in estimating what the enemy was up to, and Patton gave all the credit to Koch for his brilliance.

The American Troops

I could not be more proud of the American Army personnel, both officers and enlisted. Many of them had disrupted their private careers in defense of their country. They all performed magnificently and with a great deal of ingenuity. You must remember that when an Army increases in size as rapidly as the U.S. Army did in World War II, it is a major undertaking. Training of new personnel was often left to be acquired on the job, which frequently meant on the battleground.

In the case of the military intelligence officers and enlisted personnel, the training was particularly "spotty," few manuals existed, and there had been little hands-on experience. As with the other troops, the majority of the military intelligence personnel performed far above the expectations we had for them. It is also interesting to note that since World War II, the U.S. Army has consistently maintained a military intelligence branch—it has learned a very important lesson.

Hauenstein's Postwar Accomplishments

Chairman of Board, Lehara Corporation, New York

Special Panel Consultant to President Eisenhower (1960)

Board member of the Jamestown Foundation, Washington, D.C.

Official observer of the first popular national election in the Soviet Union (1996), as part of a Jamestown Foundation team; met with then–Soviet President Mikhail Gorbachev and other Soviet officials during that visit

Serving as observer for the 1996 Russian election. Team members: (SECOND FROM LEFT) *James Woolsey, later head of CIA;* (FOURTH FROM LEFT) *Ralph Hauenstein;* (FIFTH FROM LEFT) *Peter Cook, industrialist;* (SIXTH FROM LEFT) *Mikhail Gorbachev;* (SEVENTH FROM LEFT) *Alexander Haig, ex–Secretary of State.*

One of three board members for the establishment of the Van Andel Institute for Medical Research, Grand Rapids, Michigan

Chairman and CEO of Warner-Lehara Corporation, Grand Rapids, Michigan

Established the Hauenstein Center for Presidential Studies at Grand Valley State University, Grand Rapids, Michigan

Endowed the Hauenstein Neuroscience Center in Grand Rapids, Michigan

Lay auditor at Vatican Council II, Rome, Italy, 1964

Past international president of Serra International

Honorary trustee of the President Gerald R. Ford Foundation

Recipient of two honorary doctorates of humane letters (D.HL.)

EPILOGUE

At the age of 93, Ralph Hauenstein is still going strong. He still believes deeply in the strength of both the American people and the government of the United States. He believes that America has the ability to meet the challenges of the future and, above all, that with a good work ethic, anything is possible.

It has been a great honor for me to not only have met such a quintessential American but also to make it possible for others to "meet" a member of what has become known as the "Greatest Generation." It certainly was, as exemplified by the following speech given by Ralph Hauenstein at the 2004 Commencement Exercise for Grand Valley State University, Grand Rapids, Michigan.

* * *

Leadership and Service: What Are the Odds You Will Make a Difference?

Thank you for that kind introduction and for honoring me this day. It is especially an honor to share the day with you.

I've had the opportunity to speak with several graduating students, both here and in Florida where I spend the winter. By doing so, I hoped to gain some insight into your thoughts, your aspirations, and your view of the future.

Overall, I was encouraged. I found a strong commitment to community, a desire to contribute, and an ability to look beyond one's self to the needs of others. These are all qualities necessary for leadership and service. I also found great passion and a desire to succeed. But these later sentiments were tempered. Quite frequently I heard the comment "The odds are not good."

"The odds are not good?" My first response to that statement is, "The odds according to whom?"

I imagine if you watch the news with any regularity you have seen a rather pessimistic picture of America—both economically and as it relates to our position in the world.

But I would say to you, we have been here before. I have been here before. As many of you have astutely observed, I have a few years on you.

Along with all the little inconveniences of advancing age comes one very distinct advantage: a historic perspective. That is what I bring to you today. As both a student of and a participant in history, I encourage you to join me in examining some of the long odds throughout our country's past.

What were the odds of winning back in the 1770s, when a ragged, half-starved army under George Washington took on one of the world's superpowers, which had an army and navy far superior in numbers and professional training?

What were the odds of succeeding in the 1780s and 1790s, when our founding fathers—with little more than desire, determination, and an ideal—established a new nation, a nation that would eventually become humankind's greatest hope?

Tell me the odds of keeping our country intact in the 1860s when the North and the South could not reconcile their differences peacefully and fought each other in a civil war.

Again and again, Americans have defied the odds.

America has defied the odds because we Americans—individual citizens like you and me—have defied the odds. Those who are dedicated, who are courageous, who are visionary; those who hold fast to their ideals; those who don't lose faith—these are the Americans who make a difference, who live good lives of leadership and service.

Let me share with you a personal story. It's a wartime story and one in which the odds appeared overwhelmingly unfavorable.

In the summer of 1943—in the middle of World War II, when things were not going well for the Allies—I was assigned to London, to the United States Army's headquarters in the European Theater. It was there that we were planning a great coordinated attack on the enemy, which controlled most of the continent of Europe.

Our chances of success were small, indeed. An invading army had not crossed the English Channel since 1066—almost a thousand years. Not only did we have to cross this dangerous body of water, we had to do it with a sufficient number of troops to break through heavily fortified enemy positions. Once we broke through, we would come up against a full army with a thousand tanks and masses of heavy German artillery. How do you like those odds? Well, we didn't either. But that didn't mean we weren't obligated to try to liberate the people of Europe. British Prime Minister Winston Churchill provided a key part of our strategy in one profound statement: "In wartime, truth is far too precious not to be attended by a bodyguard of lies."

Thus was born Project BODYGUARD, a sophisticated intelligence operation that employed a myriad of highly classified activities that stretched from the Balkans to northern Norway. Once fully implemented, Project BODYGUARD became part of the famous OVER-LORD Operation.

The clever intelligence work succeeded. In the last week of May and first week of June 1944, we held an enormous army of enemy soldiers and equipment in place for 11 days. The Germans could not pinpoint where we would try to get a toehold on the continent. Their confusion enabled the Allies to land more than 150,000 men on the beaches of Normandy on June 6, 1944, thus ensuring the success of the D-day invasion.

The odds of succeeding had not been good—not at all—but we turned them in our favor. It didn't just happen. It took leaders of vision and courage—men like Prime Minister Churchill and General Eisenhower—to make it happen.

In the closing weeks of the European conflict, I was with the Allied forces on the continent. I took part in the liberation of the infamous Dachau concentration camp. I saw atrocities that I will never get out of my mind: from starving men being forced to throw the bodies of their fellow prisoners into brick ovens, to an arrogant camp commander who was seated in a room glowing with light cast through lampshades made of human skin.

The scene was unimaginably horrific. It has remained with me nearly 60 years later. But it also led to a decision point in my life.

Shortly after my discharge from the service, I returned to Europe to see how—or even if—these conquered people, whose character I questioned, could endure. I thought their odds of national survival were slim. Germany's infrastructure was in a shambles. Virtually all its industry was in ruins. Many people were half-starved and living in fear and anxiety.

But I also met people who were determined to rebuild, who possessed the vision of a peaceful, prosperous Germany in the community of nations. It was these Germans who would serve and lead the country into a better future. So I decided to work with them—and work with them in a way that would fit with American industry and markets. I'll give you an example.

While traveling through a small village in Germany, I met a man making baked goods in a small garage. Through a mostly hand-operated process, he was mixing dough and forming it into small fish-shaped snacks. Upon my return to America, I asked engineers to design equipment for mass production of a similar item. We shared our technology with the German baker, whose business grew and prospered. I then sold the equipment to a well-known American bakery, and for those of you who have ever enjoyed Goldfish crackers, you know the rest of the story.

For me, it was the beginning of a thriving import-export business. For the U.S. and Western Europe, it was a model of what could be done.

Soon, the U.S. government recognized the same needs and opportunities that we had seen, and the Marshall Plan was born. This plan was a key element in America's efforts to rebuild Western Europe and to ensure its political and economic stability. Our world is much better off because leaders back in the 1940s and 1950s ignored the odds, stuck courageously to their vision, and worked for a more peaceful, prosperous community of nations. Everyone in this room has benefited enormously from their steadfastness.

Well, that's a little history. What about the future? What about your future? What are the odds of your success?

I contend that if you are going to be a leader, if you are going to serve your community and your country, then you must not be timid or resigned to come-what-may. You must take the future into your hands to the extent that you are able. You must work to turn the odds in your favor.

Don't let yourself get down about pessimistic economic news. If the economy is going to rise out of an economic slump, all of us will have to think in new ways. Manufacturers will have to become more innovative, more creative, more efficient, and more technically savvy.

And don't forget the amazing opportunities out there—opportunities my generation never knew. A professor at Harvard Business School named Juan Enriquez recently wrote a book titled *As the Future*

Catches You. Enriquez believes the single most important discovery of the century is the sequencing of the human genome. This discovery is creating opportunities not only for scientists and mathematicians but also for artists and architects, managers and sales people, social service workers, and educators. In other words, for people with your educational backgrounds.

Not only that, but the Van Andel Institute where I serve as trustee, is the western anchor of the Michigan life sciences corridor. Grand Valley State University and President Murray are among the institute's strong local partners in building the life sciences industry here in Grand Rapids.

So opportunities are abundant—right here in this community. Don't let gloomy economic news get you down. The odds can be turned in your favor. What are needed are courageous, visionary leaders. Are you among them?

In your years of study at this university, you have acquired a foundation of knowledge and friendships that will sustain you throughout your lifetime. As to your future, I propose no nostrums, nor can I assuage any feelings of uncertainty you may have.

I can however, affirm this. Your community needs you. Our country needs you. It needs you to fulfill the hopes of your fellow citizens and to affirm the promise that is being placed in your hands—your degree.

I conclude with my congratulations. And I assure you that the odds *are* in your favor because this country offers you endless avenues of opportunity. Pursue them aggressively.

Index

Berlin, 137
Big Ben (London), 15
Bismarck, German battle cruiser, 49
Bletchley Park, 45, 55, 66n3, 79,
    84, 93–95, 111, 126–127, 154
BODYGUARD, 92
Bohr, Niels, 155
Bois de Boulogne, France, 119
Bonesteel, Charles H., 28, 29–30,
    35, 36, 38, 42, 61, 62, 80, 129
Bonesteel, Charles (Tick), 28,
    129, 130
Bornholm Island, 86
Bradley, Omar, 83, 115, 155,
    156, 160
Brandenberg Division (German
    guerilla group), 125–126
Brentano's bookstore, 29
Brest, France, 86, 87
British Guiana, 24
Brothels, 119–120
Bruce, David, 87, 89, *90*
Buck Rogers comic strip, 18
Bugle (military newspaper), 35
Bureau of Public Relations (BPR), 15
Buzz bombs, 85
Byrd, Richard, 54

Cairo Conference, 80
Calais, France, 98
Calvert, Allen, 119
Calvert, Horace K. (Tony), 96, 97,
    126, 127, 155, 156
Camp Bitely, 8–9
Camp Pershing, Iceland, 34
Canada, 68, 82
Canaris, Wilhelm C., 125–126
Cannes, France, 120, 123
Carlton Hotel, 123
Carpentier, George, 118
Carter, Jimmy, 147n3
Cavendish House Hotel, 103,
    104, 105

Cemeteries, 59, 66n4
Central Intelligence Agency (CIA),
    83, 84, 154
Chaney, James E., 69, 70
Channel Islands, 111
Chapman, Fred A., 66n5
Chevalier, Maurice, 117
Chicago Daily News (Illinois), 4
Chicago Tribune (Illinois), 15
Christian Science Monitor, 4
Churchill, Winston, 69, 154,
    155, 167
Civilian Conservation Corps
    (CCC), 7–11
Claussen, Henry C., 150, 151
Clay, Lucius D., 152
COBWEB, German double agent,
    59–60, 63, 92
Coca-Cola representatives, 116, 124n
Code breakers, 55, 79, 93–94,
    100n1, 111, 126–127
Coke Goes To War, 124n
Combined Operations School, 81
Combined Strategic Targets
    Committee, 110
Commencement speech, Grand
    Valley State University,
    165–169
Committee of Twenty, 95
Communications Zone (COM Z),
    74–76, 120
Concentration camps, 130, 132,
    133–136, 137
Confrere de Notre Dame, 117
Conrad, Bryan, 77, 79, 97, 129
Cook, Peter, *163*
Corpses of male prisoners,
    Dachau, *135*
COSSAC (Chief of Staff, Supreme
    Allied Command), 68, 73,
    78–80
Counter Intelligence Corps
    (CIC), 110

Acknowledgments

Donald E. Markle

This book would not have been written if it had not been for Paul Nelson, president emeritus of Aquinas College in Grand Rapids, Michigan, and I am truly grateful for his initiative.

Paul Nelson was a student of mine in an Elderhostel class in Gettysburg. I was teaching a course called "The History of U.S. Intelligence," and after the second day he approached me and told me he knew someone "I needed to talk to." He explained that a man by the name of Ralph W. Hauenstein, a resident of Grand Rapids, had been involved in intelligence work during World War II and had never spoken to anyone about what he did during that time. My immediate response was "Yes!" I would love to meet the man and talk with him about his experiences. And so this book was born.

I traveled to Grand Rapids to meet with Mr. Hauenstein to discuss his World War II experiences. He opened up to me immediately, probably because, I, too, had spent many years in the intelligence business, and we soon decided to undertake a book that would serve two purposes. First, it would further educate readers on the role of intelligence during World War II; second, Mr. Hauenstein felt strongly that the role of the European Theater of Operations U.S. Army (ETOUSA) had never been clearly understood by either the lay reader or the military historian. He hopes we can correct that.

Ralph himself, credits a good friend Peter Wege, also a World War II veteran and fellow resident of Grand Rapids for making the book happen. For years Peter kept prodding him to record his World War II experiences, to no avail until now—persistence finally paid off.

My work was made easier by the cooperation of the entire Hauenstein family, who backed the project wholeheartedly. They, too, were learning about what their father (and to some, their grandfather and great-grandfather) had done during his time in World War II.

The project got a boost from the Eisenhower Society of Gettysburg, Pennsylvania, which awarded me a small grant to cover the travel expenses for my initial trip to Grand Rapids. I am truly grateful for their support.

In the course of the research for the book, the following were helpful and I am grateful to them: the staffs of the National Archives at College Park, Maryland, both in the records and photographic areas; the staff of the U.S. Army War College in Carlisle, Pennsylvania; and the staff of the Adams Country Library System in Gettysburg, Pennsylvania, who never failed to respond to my many and varied requests.

Kris Driscoll of Bare Hands Design was of great assistance in developing the specific maps that add a great deal to the understanding of the text.

I would be remiss if I did not mention three very special people. First, my wife, Geri, who supported the project from the onset. She is one tough editor, which I need and value. Second, Art Thimsen, a fellow colleague from the intelligence world, who served as my frequent sounding board and technical advisor. He is a great detail man! And last but not least, Antigoni Ladd, who served as my unofficial editor, and her assistant Camie Stouch, who provided computer support, particularly with the photographs.

But the main person I have to thank for this publication is the man himself, Ralph W. Hauenstein, who opened his memory bank to me. He was a joy to work with throughout the project—always willing to dig a little deeper and always very precise in relating his experiences. He is a great example of what America is all about and what a person can accomplish when called upon.

Finally, to Hippocrene Books, who saw the historic value of the work, and to Tatiana Shohov, the editor who carried the project through to completion.

—Donald E. Markle
Gettysburg, Pennsylvania, 2005

Military Intelligence from Hippocrene Books

Spies & Spymasters of the Civil War, Revised & Expanded Edition
Donald Markle, co-author of Intelligence Was My Line

> "For his complete account of the subject, Markle draws upon just about all the available material and summarizes it with judgment, balance, clarity, and occasional wit."
> —*Booklist*

> ". . . a marvelous book. It weaves an intertwined yet easy to understand perspective of people, places, organizations, secret societies, politics, and the vehicles of spy craft during an unprecedented time of upheaval in our country's history."
> —*The Midwest Book Review*

Now with a new chapter on American espionage after the Civil War, this book covers the entire history of Civil War espionage for both the Union and Confederate armies. The activities and tactics of hundreds of spies are described, including spymasters who controlled spy networks, like Allan Pinkerton, Lafayette Baker, and Generals Dodge, Sharpe, and Garfield. The book also examines the role of the Negro underground organizations and women spies.

270 pages • 8-page b/w photo insert • ISBN 0-7818-0761-1 • $14.95 pb • (622)

Enigma: How the Poles Broke the Nazi Code
Władysław Kozaczuk and Jerzy Straszak

The decipherment of the German military code Enigma remains one of the most exciting—yet little known—stories of World War II. The Polish cryptographers who cracked it in 1933 and shared their knowledge with French and British intelligence services in 1939 have only recently received international recognition for their efforts. This concise history of the Enigma decryption and its uses also includes several essays on the subject and over 60 black-and-white illustrations.

"Poland did what no other country had done—and what Germans themselves considered impossible. They deserve thanks for the great Polish solution that saved so many lives and did so much good for the world."

—David Kahn, author of
Seizing the Enigma

165 pages • over 60 photos and illustrations • ISBN 0-7818-0941-X • $22.50 hc • (294)

Hippocrene Books, Inc.
171 Madison Avenue, New York, NY 10016
www.hippocrenebooks.com
order by phone: 718-454-2366